KENNETH & GLORIA COPELAND

HEALING
PROMISES

KENNETH
COPELAND
PUBLICATIONS

Healing Promises

ISBN-10: 0-88114-949-7   30-0701
ISBN-13: 978-0-88114-949-4

19 18 17 16 15 14   22 21 20 19 18 17

Kenneth Copeland Publications
Fort Worth, TX 76192-0001

For more information about Kenneth Copeland Ministries, visit kcm.org or call 1-800-600-7395 (U.S. only) or +1-817-852-6000.

F O R E W O R D

"Who his own self bare our sins in his own
body on the tree, that we, being dead to
sins, should live unto righteousness: by
whose stripes ye were healed"
(1 Peter 2:24).

When Gloria and I first heard this scripture taught years ago, we believed in healing. We even believed God's will was for people to be healed. Yet sometimes we got healed and sometimes we didn't.

But let me tell you, the day we found out Jesus had already done the work and healing belonged to us—that we were no longer the sick trying to get healed—we started believing and acting like the healed and haven't stopped since. Glory to God!

You know, you could go out and ask believers all day long, "Do you believe God can heal you?" and most would probably say "Oh, yes!" But ask them if God will heal them and you're likely to hear, "Well, I guess...oh, I know He could, but I'm just not sure...."

Well praise God, there's no reason to wonder anymore! God is the "Father of lights, with whom is no variableness, neither shadow of turning" (James 1:17). God has not changed. He healed in the Old Testament, He healed in the New, and He heals today. Hallelujah!

The Word says in Proverbs 4:20-22:

"My son, attend to my words; incline thine ear unto
my sayings. Let them not depart from thine eyes;
keep them in the midst of thine heart. For they are
life unto those that find them, and health to all
their flesh."

Gloria and I have never had a single healing service where God failed to heal and deliver His people. That's because we have always preached the Word and relied on the Name of Jesus and the Holy Spirit to break the yoke of bondage—sin, sickness, disease and death.

Anywhere, at any time, the Spirit of God is always ready to heal. And whether you're in the last stages of cancer or just have a headache, healing is yours the moment you make a demand on it. But for God's healing to manifest, He needs faith—*your* faith.

That's why we have put together this book of *Healing Promises*. We want to help you get the truth about healing established in your heart, and to help you keep God's Word before you all the time.

Read *Healing Promises* over and over. As you do, the Word will increase your faith and erase any doubt from your heart. Then apply your faith to God's healing promises.They will become life to you, and health to all your flesh.

The words of God are God's medicine. You don't have to be concerned about an overdose. The more you take, the better you are!

Kenneth and Gloria Copeland

TABLE OF CONTENTS

1

Healing Is
God's Will

*God is a good God, and
it is His very nature to
heal. From beginning to
end, the Bible makes it
clear that it has always
been God's will to heal
His people.*

Exodus 15:26

KJV—If thou wilt diligently hearken to the voice of the Lord thy God, and wilt do that which is right in his sight, and wilt give ear to his commandments, and keep all his statutes, I will put none of these diseases upon thee, which I have brought upon the Egyptians: for I am the Lord that healeth thee.

Amp—If you will diligently hearken to the voice of the Lord your God, and will do what is right in His sight, and will listen to and obey His commandments and keep all His statutes, I will put none of the diseases upon you which I brought upon the Egyptians; for I am the Lord Who heals you.

Moffatt—If you will listen carefully to the voice of the Eternal, your God, and do what is right in his eyes and pay heed to his commands and follow all his rules, then the Eternal promises never to inflict upon you any of the diseases he inflicted on the Egyptians; for he is the Eternal who heals you.

NEB—If only you will obey the Lord your God, if you will do what is right in his eyes, if you will listen to his commands and keep all his statutes, then I will never bring upon you any of the sufferings which I brought on the Egyptians; for I the Lord am your healer.

Exodus 23:25

KJV—And ye shall serve the Lord your God, and he shall bless thy bread, and thy water; and I will take sickness away from the midst of thee.

Amp—You shall serve the Lord your God; He shall bless your bread and water, and I will take sickness from your midst.

Moffatt—You shall worship the Eternal your God, and then I will bless your food and water, and I will free you from disease.

NEB—Worship the Lord your God, and he will bless your bread and your water. I will take away all sickness out of your midst.

Deuteronomy 7:14-15

KJV—Thou shalt be blessed above all people: there shall not be male or female barren among you, or among your cattle. And the Lord will take away from thee all sickness, and will put none of the evil diseases of Egypt, which thou knowest, upon thee; but will lay them upon all them that hate thee.

Amp—You shall be blessed above all peoples; there shall not be male or female barren among you, or among your cattle. And the Lord will take away from you all sickness, and none of the evil diseases of Egypt, which you knew, will He put upon you, but will lay them upon all who hate you.

Moffatt—You shall have more prosperity than any nation; not a male or female shall be barren among you or among your cattle. The Eternal will also free you from all sickness; he will not inflict upon you any of the evil diseases of Egypt which you know so well, but will inflict them upon all who hate you.

NEB—You shall be blessed above every other nation; neither among your people nor among your cattle shall there be impotent male or barren female. The Lord will take away all sickness from you; he will not bring upon you any of the foul diseases of Egypt which you know so well, but will bring them upon all your enemies.

Deuteronomy 28:1-14

KJV—And it shall come to pass, if thou shalt hearken diligently unto the voice of the Lord thy God, to observe and to do all his commandments which I command thee this day, that the Lord thy God will set thee on high above all nations of the earth: And all these blessings shall come on thee, and overtake thee, if thou shalt hearken unto the voice of the Lord thy God.

Blessed shalt thou be in the city, and blessed shalt thou be in the field. Blessed shall be the fruit of thy body, and the fruit of thy ground, and the fruit of thy cattle, the increase of thy kine, and the flocks of thy sheep. Blessed shall be thy basket and thy store. Blessed shalt thou be when thou comest in, and blessed shalt thou be when thou goest out.

The Lord shall cause thine enemies that rise up against thee to be smitten before thy face: they shall come out against thee one way, and flee before thee seven ways. The Lord shall command the blessing upon thee in thy storehouses, and in all that thou settest thine hand unto; and he shall bless thee in the land which the Lord thy God giveth thee.

The Lord shall establish thee an holy people unto himself, as he hath sworn unto thee, if thou shalt keep the commandments of the Lord thy God, and walk in his ways. And all people of the earth shall see that thou art called by the name of the Lord; and they shall be afraid of thee.

And the Lord shall make thee plenteous in goods, in the fruit of thy body, and in the fruit of thy cattle, and in the fruit of thy ground, in the land which the Lord sware unto thy fathers to give thee. The Lord shall open unto thee his good treasure, the heaven to give the rain unto thy land in his season, and to bless all the work of thine hand: and thou shalt lend unto many nations, and thou shalt not borrow.

And the Lord shall make thee the head, and not the tail; and thou shalt be above only, and thou shalt not be beneath; if that thou hearken unto the commandments of the Lord thy God, which I command thee this day, to observe and to do them: And thou shalt not go aside from any of the words which I command thee this day, to the right hand, or to the left, to go after other gods to serve them.

Amp—If you will listen diligently to the voice of the Lord your God, being watchful to do all His commandments which I command you this day, the Lord your God will set you high above all the nations of the earth, And all these blessings shall come upon you and overtake you, if you heed the voice of the Lord your God.

Blessed shall you be in the city, and blessed shall you be in the field. Blessed shall be the fruit of your body, and the fruit of your ground, and the fruit of your beasts, the increase of your cattle, and the young of your flock. Blessed shall be your basket and your kneading trough. Blessed shall you be when you come in, and blessed shall you be when you go out.

The Lord shall cause your enemies who rise up against you to be defeated before your face; they shall come out against you one way, and flee before you seven ways. The Lord shall command the blessing upon you in your storehouse, and in all that you undertake; and he will bless you in the land which the Lord your God gives you.

The Lord will establish you as a people holy to Himself, as He has sworn to you, if you keep the commandments of the Lord your God, and walk in His ways. And all people of the earth shall see that you are called by the name [and in the presence of] the Lord; and they shall be afraid of you.

And the Lord shall make you have a surplus of prosperity, through the fruit of your body, of your livestock, and of your ground, in the land which the Lord swore to your fathers to give you. The Lord shall open to you His good treasury, the heavens to give the rain of your land in its season, and to bless all the work of your hand; and you shall lend to many nations, but you shall not borrow.

And the Lord shall make you the head, and not the tail; and you shall be above only, and you shall not be beneath, if you heed the commandments of the Lord your God, which I command you this day, and are watchful to do them. And you shall not go aside from any of the words which I command you this day, to the right hand or to the left, to go after other gods to serve them.

Moffatt—If only you will listen carefully to what the Eternal your God orders, mindful to carry out all his commands which I enjoin upon you this day, then the Eternal your God will lift you high above all the nations of the earth, and all these blessings shall come upon you and overtake you, if only you listen to the voice of the Eternal your God.

You shall be blessed in town and in country; blessed shall be the fruit of your body and of your ground, the young of your cattle and the lambs of your flock; full shall your basket be, and your kneading-trough; blessed shall you be as you start out and as you come home.

The foes who attack you the Eternal will rout before you; they may assail you all together, but they shall fly before you in all directions. The Eternal will command you to be blessed in your barns and in every enterprise to which you put your hand, blessing you in the land which the Eternal your God assigns to you.

The Eternal will confirm your position as a people sacred to himself, as he swore to you, if you obey the orders of the Eternal your God and live his life, so that when all nations on earth see you are owned by the Eternal, they may stand in awe of you.

The Eternal will make you overflow with prosperity in the fruit of your body, of your cattle, and of your ground, the ground that the Eternal swore to your fathers that he would give you. The Eternal will open his rich treasury of heaven for you, to bestow rain in due season on your land, blessing all your labours, so that you shall lend to many a nation but never need to borrow from them.

So shall the Eternal put you at the head, not at the tail; you shall be always rising, never falling, as you listen to the commands of the Eternal your God which I enjoin upon you this day, and carry them out carefully, never swerving to right or to left from any of the injunctions I lay upon you this day, by going after any other gods to worship them.

NEB—If you will obey the Lord your God by diligently observing all his commandments which I lay upon you this day, then the Lord your God will raise you high above all nations of the earth, and all these blessings shall come to you and light upon you, because you obey the Lord your God:

A blessing on you in the city; a blessing on you in the country. A blessing on the fruit of your body, the fruit of your land and of your cattle, the offspring of your herds and of your lambing flocks. A blessing on your basket and your kneading-trough. A blessing on you as you come in; and blessing on you as you go out.

May the Lord deliver up the enemies who attack you and let them be put to rout before you. Though they come out against you by one way, they shall flee before you by seven ways. May the Lord grant you a blessing in your granaries and in all your labours; may the Lord your God bless you in the land which he is giving you.

The Lord will set you up as his own holy people, as he swore to you, if you keep the commandments of the Lord your God and conform to his ways. Then all people on earth shall see that the Lord has named you as his very own, and they shall go in fear of you.

The Lord will make you prosper greatly in the fruit of your body and of your cattle, and in the fruit of the ground in the land which he swore to your forefathers to give you. May the Lord open the heavens for you, his rich treasure house, to give rain upon your land at the proper time and bless everything to which you turn your hand. You shall lend to many nations, but you shall not borrow;

The Lord will make you the head and not the tail: you shall be always at the top and never at the bottom, when you listen to the commandments of the Lord your God, which I give you this day to keep and to fulfil. You shall turn neither to the right nor to the left from all the things which I command you this day nor shall you follow after and worship other gods.

Deuteronomy 30:19-20

KJV—I call heaven and earth to record this day against you, that I have set before you life and death, blessing and cursing: therefore choose life, that both thou and thy seed may live: That thou mayest love the Lord thy God, and that thou mayest obey his voice, and that thou mayest cleave unto him: for he is thy life, and the length of thy days: that thou mayest dwell in the land which the Lord sware unto thy fathers, to Abraham, to Isaac, and to Jacob, to give them.

Amp—I call Heaven and earth to witness this day against you, that I have set before you life and death, the blessing and the curse; therefore choose life, that you and your descendants may live; To love the Lord your God, to obey His voice, and to cling to Him; for He is your life, and the length of your days, that you may dwell in the land which the Lord swore to give to your fathers, to Abraham, Isaac, and Jacob.

Moffatt—Here and now I call heaven and earth to witness against you that I have put life and death before you, the blessing and the curse: choose life, then, that you and your children may live, by loving the Eternal your God, obeying his voice, and holding fast to him, for that means life to you and length of days, that you may live in the land which the Eternal swore to Abraham, Isaac, and Jacob, your fathers, that he would give to them.

NEB—I summon heaven and earth to witness against you this day: I offer you the choice of life or death, blessing or curse. Choose life and then you and your descendants will live; love the Lord your God, obey him and hold fast to him: that is life for you and length of days in the land which the Lord swore to give to your forefathers, Abraham, Isaac and Jacob.

Joshua 21:45

KJV—There failed not aught of any good thing which the Lord had spoken unto the house of Israel; all came to pass.

Amp—There failed no part of any good thing which the Lord had promised to the house of Israel; all came to pass.

Moffatt—Not one of the good promises made by the Eternal to the house of Israel failed; all were fulfilled.

NEB—Not a word of the Lord's promises to the house of Israel went unfulfilled; they all came true.

1 Kings 8:56

KJV—Blessed be the Lord, that hath given rest unto his people Israel, according to all that he promised: there hath not failed one word of all his good promise, which he promised by the hand of Moses his servant.

Amp—Blessed be the Lord Who has given rest to His people Israel, according to all that He promised. Not one word has failed of all His good promise which He promised through Moses His servant.

Moffatt—Blessed be the Eternal who has granted rest to his people Israel, as he promised; not a word has failed of all the good promises he made to us by Moses his servant.

NEB—Blessed be the Lord who has given his people Israel rest, as he promised: not one of the promises he made through his servant Moses has failed.

Psalm 34:19

KJV—Many are the afflictions of the righteous: but the Lord delivereth him out of them all.

Amp—Many evils confront the [consistently] righteous; but the Lord delivers him out of them all.

Moffatt—The good man may have many a mishap, but from them all the Eternal rescues him.

NEB—The good man's misfortunes may be many, the Lord delivers him out of them all.

Psalm 91:9-10, 14-16

KJV—Because thou hast made the Lord, which is my refuge, even the most High, thy habitation; there shall no evil befall thee, neither shall any plague come nigh thy dwelling...Because he hath set his love upon me, therefore will I deliver him: I will set him on high, because he hath known my name. He shall call upon me, and I will answer him: I will be with him in trouble; I will deliver him, and honour him. With long life will I satisfy him, and show him my salvation.

Amp—Because you have made the Lord your refuge, and the Most High your dwelling place, There shall no evil befall you, nor any plague or calamity come near your tent...Because he has set his love upon Me, therefore will I deliver him; I will set him on high, because he knows and understands My name [has a personal knowledge of My mercy, love and kindness; trusts and relies on Me, knowing I will never forsake him, no, never]. He shall call upon Me, and I will answer him; I will be with him in trouble, I will deliver him and honor him. With long life will I satisfy him, and show him My salvation.

Moffatt—But you have sheltered beside the Eternal, and made the Most High God your home, so no scathe can befall you, no plague can approach your tent...He clings to me, so I deliver him; I set him safe, because he cares for me; I will answer his cry and be with him in trouble, delivering him and honouring him; I will satisfy him with long life, and let him see my saving care.

NEB—For you, the Lord is a safe retreat; you have made the Most High your refuge. No disaster shall befall you, no calamity shall come upon your home. Because his love is set on me, I will deliver him; I will lift him beyond danger, for he knows me by my name. When he calls upon me, I will answer; I will be with him in time of trouble; I will rescue him and bring him to honour. I will satisfy him with long life to enjoy the fullness of my salvation.

Psalm 103:1-5

KJV—Bless the Lord, O my soul: and all that is within me, bless his holy name. Bless the Lord, O my soul, and forget not all his benefits: Who forgiveth all thine iniquities; who healeth all thy diseases; Who redeemeth thy life from destruction; who crowneth thee with lovingkindness and tender mercies; Who satisfieth thy mouth with good things; so that thy youth is renewed like the eagle's.

Amp—Bless—affectionately, gratefully praise—the Lord, O

my soul, and all that is [deepest] within me, bless His holy name! Bless—affectionately, gratefully praise—the Lord, O my soul, and forget not [one of] all His benefits, Who forgives [every one of] all your iniquities, Who heals [each of] all your diseases; Who redeems your life from the pit and corruption; Who beautifies, dignifies and crowns you with loving-kindness and tender mercies; Who satisfies your mouth [your necessity and desire at your personal age] with good; so that your youth, renewed, is like the eagle's [strong, overcoming, soaring]!

Moffatt—Bless the Eternal, O my soul, let all my being bless his sacred name; bless the Eternal, O my soul, remember all his benefits; he pardons all your sins, and all your sicknesses he heals, he saves your life from death, he crowns you with his love and pity, he gives you all your heart's desire, renewing your youth like an eagle's.

NEB—Bless the Lord, my soul; my innermost heart, bless his holy name. Bless the Lord, my soul, and forget none of his benefits. He pardons all my guilt and heals all my suffering. He rescues me from the pit of death and surrounds me with constant love, with tender affection; he contents me with all good in the prime of life, and my youth is ever new like an eagle's.

Psalm 107:19-21

KJV—Then they cry unto the Lord in their trouble, and he saveth them out of their distresses. He sent his word, and healed them, and delivered them from their destructions. Oh that men would praise the Lord for his goodness, and for his wonderful works to the children of men!

Amp—Then they cry to the Lord in their trouble, and He delivers them out of their distresses. He sends forth His word and heals them and rescues them from the pit and destruction. Oh, that men would praise [and confess to] the Lord His goodness and loving-kindness, and His wonderful works to the children of men!

Moffatt—They cried to the Eternal in their need, to save them from their evil plight; he sent his word to heal them and preserve their life. Let them thank the Eternal for his kindness, and for the wonders that he does for men.

NEB—So they cried to the Lord in their trouble, and he saved them from their distress; he sent his word to heal them and bring them alive out of the pit of death. Let them thank the Lord for his enduring love and for the marvellous things he has done for men.

Psalm 118:17

KJV—I shall not die, but live, and declare the works of the Lord.

Amp—I shall not die, but live, and declare the works and recount the illustrious acts of the Lord.

Moffatt—I shall not die, but live to proclaim the Eternal's deeds.

NEB—I shall not die but live to proclaim the works of the Lord.

Isaiah 40:28-31

KJV—Hast thou not known? hast thou not heard, that the everlasting God, the Lord, the Creator of the ends of the earth, fainteth not, neither is weary? there is no searching of his understanding. He giveth power to the faint; and to them that have no might he increaseth strength. Even the youths shall faint and be weary, and the young men shall utterly fall: But they that wait upon the Lord shall renew their strength; they shall mount up with wings as eagles; they shall run, and not be weary; and they shall walk, and not faint.

Amp—Have you not known? Have you not heard? The everlasting God, the Lord, the Creator of the ends of the earth, does not faint or grow weary; there is no searching of His understanding. He gives power to the faint and weary, and to him who has no might He increases strength—causing it to multiply and making it abound. Even youths shall faint and be weary, and the selected young men shall feebly stumble and fall exhausted; But those who wait for the Lord—who expect, look for and hope in Him—shall change and renew their strength and power; they shall lift their wings and mount up [close to God] as eagles [mount up to the sun]; they shall run and not be weary; they shall walk and not faint or become tired.

Moffatt—Come now! Do you not understand, have you not heard, that the Eternal is an everlasting God, the maker of the world from end to end? He never faints, never is weary, his insight is unsearchable; into the weary he puts power, and adds new strength to the weak. Young men may faint and weary, the strong youths may give way, but those who wait for the Eternal shall renew their strength, they put out wings like eagles, they run and never weary, they walk and never faint.

NEB—Do you not know, have you not heard? The Lord, the everlasting God, creator of the wide world, grows neither weary nor faint; no man can fathom his understanding. He gives vigour to the weary, new strength to the exhausted. Young men may grow weary and faint, even in their prime they may stumble and fall; but those who look to the Lord will win new strength, they will grow wings like eagles; they will run and not be weary, they will march on and never grow faint.

Isaiah 41:10

KJV—Fear thou not; for I am with thee: be not dismayed; for I am thy God: I will strengthen thee; yea, I will help thee; yea, I will uphold thee with the right hand of my righteousness.

Amp—Fear not; [there is nothing to fear] for I am with you; do not look around you in terror and be dismayed, for I am your God. I will strengthen and harden you [to difficulties]; yes, I will help you; yes, I will hold you up and retain you with My victorious right hand of rightness and justice.

Moffatt—Fear not, for I am with you, I am your God, be not dismayed; I will strengthen, I will support you, I will uphold you with my trusty hand.

NEB—Fear nothing, for I am with you; be not afraid, for I am your God. I strengthen you, I help you, I support you with my victorious right hand.

Jeremiah 1:12

KJV—Then said the Lord unto me, Thou hast well seen: for I will hasten my word to perform it.

Amp—Then said the Lord to me, You have seen well, for I am alert and active, watching over My word to perform it.

Moffatt—The Eternal said to me, You have seen right; for I am wakeful over my word, to carry it out.

NEB—You are right, said the Lord to me, for I am early on the watch to carry out my purpose.

Jeremiah 30:17

KJV—For I will restore health unto thee, and I will heal thee of thy wounds, saith the Lord; because they called thee an

Outcast, saying, This is Zion, whom no man seeketh after.

Amp—For I will restore health to you, and I will heal your wounds, says the Lord; because they have called you an outcast, saying, This is Zion, whom no one seeks after and for whom no one cares!

Moffatt—For I will give you health again, and heal your wounds, the Eternal promises—you whom the hunters called an outcast, Our quarry! No one cares for her!

NEB—I will cause the new skin to grow and heal your wounds, says the Lord, although men call you the Outcast, Zion, nobody's friend.

Nahum 1:9

KJV—What do ye imagine against the Lord? he will make an utter end: affliction shall not rise up the second time.

Amp—What do you devise and [how mad is your attempt to] plot against the Lord? He will make a full end of Nineveh; affliction [which My people shall suffer from Assyria] shall not rise up the second time.

Moffatt—He has not to take vengeance twice upon his foes, he makes an end of them. Why plot against the Eternal?

NEB—No adversaries dare oppose him twice; all are burnt up like tangled briars. Why do you make plots against the Lord?

Malachi 4:2

KJV—But unto you that fear my name shall the Sun of righteousness arise with healing in his wings; and ye shall go forth, and grow up as calves of the stall.

Amp—But unto you who revere and worshipfully fear My name shall the Sun of righteousness arise with healing in His wings and His beams, and you shall go forth and gambol like calves released from the stall and leap for joy.

Moffatt—But for you, my worshipers, the saving Sun shall rise with healing in his rays, and you shall leap like calves freed from the pen.

NEB—But for you who fear my name, the sun of righteousness shall rise with healing in his wings, and you shall break loose like calves released from the stall.

Philippians 2:13

KJV—For it is God which worketh in you both to will and to do of his good pleasure.

Amp—[Not in your own strength] for it is God Who is all the while effectually at work in you—energizing and creating in you the power and desire—both to will and to work for His good pleasure and satisfaction and delight.

Moffatt—For it is God who in his goodwill enables you to will this and to achieve it.

NEB—For it is God who works in you, inspiring both the will and the deed, for his own chosen purpose.

* * *

Healing in Redemption

Healing is more than God's will, it is His provision. The price for your healing was paid at Calvary—it is part of your redemption.

John 10:10

KJV—The thief cometh not, but for to steal, and to kill, and to destroy: I am come that they might have life, and that they might have it more abundantly.

Amp—The thief comes only in order that he may steal and may kill and may destroy. I came that they may have and enjoy life, and have it in abundance—to the full, till it overflows.

Moffatt—The thief only comes to steal, to slay, and to destroy: I have come that they may have life and have it to the full.

NEB—The thief comes only to steal, to kill, to destroy; I have come that men may have life, and may have it in all its fullness.

Isaiah 53:4-5

KJV—Surely he hath borne our griefs, and carried our sorrows: yet we did esteem him stricken, smitten of God, and afflicted. But he was wounded for our transgressions, he was bruised for our iniquities: the chastisement of our peace was upon him; and with his stripes we are healed.

Amp—Surely He has borne our griefs—sickness, weakness and distress—and carried our sorrows and pain [of punishment]. Yet we ignorantly considered Him stricken, smitten and afflicted by God [as if with leprosy]. But He was wounded for our transgressions, He was bruised for our guilt and iniquities; the chastisement needful to obtain peace and well-being for us was upon Him, and with the stripes that wounded Him we are healed and made whole.

Moffatt—And yet ours was the pain he bore, the sorrow he endured! We thought him suffering from a stroke at God's own hand; yet he was wounded because we had sinned, 'twas our misdeeds that crushed him; 'twas for our welfare that he was chastised, the blows that fell to him have brought us healing.

NEB—Yet on himself he bore our sufferings, our torments he endured, while we counted him smitten by God, struck down by disease and misery; but he was pierced for our transgressions, tortured for our iniquities; the chastisement he bore is health for us and by his scourging we are healed.

1 Peter 2:24

KJV—Who his own self bare our sins in his own body on the tree, that we, being dead to sins, should live unto righteousness: by whose stripes ye were healed.

Amp—He personally bore our sins in His [own] body to the tree [as to an altar and offered Himself on it], that we might die (cease to exist) to sin and live to righteousness. By His wounds you have been healed.

Moffatt—He bore our sins in his own body on the gibbet, that we might break with sin and live the good life; it is by his wounds that you have been healed.

NEB—In his own person he carried our sins to the gibbet, so that we might cease to live for sin and begin to live for righteousness. By his wounds you have been healed.

Isaiah 54:8-17

KJV—In a little wrath I hid my face from thee for a moment; but with everlasting kindness will I have mercy on thee, saith the Lord thy Redeemer. For this is as the waters of Noah unto me: for as I have sworn that the waters of Noah should no more go over the earth; so have I sworn that I would not be wroth with thee, nor rebuke thee. For the mountains shall depart, and the hills be removed; but my kindness shall not depart from thee, neither shall the covenant of my peace be removed, saith the Lord that hath mercy on thee.

O thou afflicted, tossed with tempest, and not comforted, behold, I will lay thy stones with fair colours, and lay thy foundations with sapphires. And I will make thy windows of agates, and thy gates of carbuncles, and all thy borders of pleasant stones. And all thy children shall be taught of the Lord; and great shall be the peace of thy children.

In righteousness shalt thou be established: thou shalt be far from oppression; for thou shalt not fear: and from terror; for it shall not come near thee. Behold, they shall surely gather together, but not by me: whosoever shall gather together against thee shall fall for thy sake. Behold, I have created the smith that bloweth the coals in the fire, and that bringeth forth an instrument for his work; and I have created the waster (that) destroys.

No weapon that is formed against thee shall prosper; and every tongue that shall rise against thee in judgment thou shalt condemn. This is the heritage of the servants of the Lord, and their righteousness is of me, saith the Lord.

Amp—In a little burst of wrath I hid My face from you for a moment, but with age-enduring love and kindness I will have compassion and mercy on you, says the Lord, your Redeemer. For this is as the days of Noah to Me; as I have sworn that the waters of Noah should no more go over the earth, so have I sworn that I will not be angry with you or rebuke you. For though the mountains should depart and the hills be shaken or removed, yet My love and kindness shall not depart from you, nor shall My covenant of peace and completeness be removed, says the Lord, Who has compassion on you.

O you afflicted, storm-tossed and not comforted, behold, I will set your stones in fair colors—in antimony [to enhance their brilliance]—and lay your foundations with sapphires. And I will make your windows and pinnacles of [sparkling] agates or rubies, and your gates of [shining] carbuncles, and all the walls of your enclosures of precious stones. And all your [spiritual] children shall be disciples—taught of the Lord [and obedient to His will]; and great shall be the peace and undisturbed composure of your children.

You shall establish yourself on righteousness—right, in conformity with God's will and order; you shall be far even from the thought of oppression or destruction, for you shall not fear; and from terror, for it shall not come near you. Behold, they may gather together and stir up strife, but it is not from Me. Whoever stirs up strife against you shall fall away to you. Behold, I have created the smith who blows on the fire of coals, and who produces a weapon for its purpose, and I have created the devastator to destroy.

But no weapon that is formed against you shall prosper, and every tongue that shall rise against you in judgment you shall show to be in the wrong. This [peace, righteousness, security, triumph over opposition] is the heritage of the servants of the Lord [those in whom the ideal Servant of the Lord is reproduced]. This is the righteousness or the vindication which they obtain from Me—this is that which I impart to them as their justification—says the Lord.

Moffatt—I did turn from you in a rush of wrath, but with a lasting love I pity you: so promises the Eternal your redeemer. 'Tis like the days of Noah; for as then I swore that Noah's waters should flood earth no more, so now I swear that nevermore will I rebuke you in my wrath. Though mountains be removed, and hills be shaken, never shall my love leave you, my compact for your welfare shall stand firm: so promises the Eternal in his pity.

Poor storm-tossed soul, disconsolate, I will build you up on jewels. and make sapphires your foundation; I will make ramparts out of rubies, gates for you of crystals, and all your walls of gems; the Eternal will train all your builders, and prosper your sons mightily; your triumph shall be stable.

Oppression shall be far from you, and nothing need you fear; ruin shall be remote from you, it never shall come near. Should strife be stirred, 'tis not by me; whoever falls on you shall fall to ruin. 'Tis I, I make the smith who heats his furnace, and fashions weapons by his craft; 'tis I who make destroyers to destroy.

No weapon forged against you shall succeed, no tongue raised against you shall win its plea. Such is the lot of the Eternal's servants; thus, the Eternal promises, do I maintain their cause.

NEB—In sudden anger I hid my face from you for a moment; but now have I pitied you with a love which never fails, says the Lord who ransoms you. These days recall for me the days of Noah: as I swore that the waters of Noah's flood should never again pour over the earth, so now I swear to you never again to be angry with you or reproach you. Though the mountains move and the hills shake, my love shall be immovable and never fail, and my covenant of peace shall not be shaken. So says the Lord who takes pity on you.

O storm-battered city, distressed and disconsolate, now I will set your stones in the finest mortar and your foundations in lapis lazuli; I will make your battlements of red jasper and your gates of garnet; all your boundary-stones shall be jewels. Your masons shall all be instructed by the Lord, and your sons shall enjoy great prosperity; and in triumph shall you be restored.

You shall be free from oppression and have no fears, free from terror, and it shall not come near you; should any attack you, it will not be my doing, the aggressor, whoever he be, shall perish for his attempt. It was I who created the smith to fan the coals in the furnace and forge weapons each for its purpose, and I who created the destroyer to lay waste; but now no weapon made to harm you shall prevail, and you shall rebut every charge brought against you. Such is the fortune of the servants of the Lord; their vindication comes from me. This is the very word of the Lord.

Revelation 21:4

KJV—And God shall wipe away all tears from their eyes; and there shall be no more death, neither sorrow, nor crying, neither shall there be any more pain: for the former things are passed away.

Amp—God will wipe away every tear from their eyes, and death shall be no more, neither shall there be anguish—sorrow and mourning—nor grief nor pain any more; for the old conditions and the former order of things have passed way.

Moffatt—He shall wipe every tear from their eyes, and death shall be no more—no more wailing, no more crying, no more pain, for the former things have passed away.

NEB—He will wipe every tear from their eyes; there shall be an end to death, and to mourning and crying and pain; for the old order has passed away!

Deuteronomy 28:15, 22, 27-28, 35, 58-61

KJV—But it shall come to pass, if thou wilt not hearken unto the voice of the Lord thy God, to observe to do all his commandments and his statutes which I command thee this day; that all these curses shall come upon thee, and overtake thee.

The Lord shall smite thee with a consumption, and with a fever, and with an inflammation, and with an extreme burning, and with the sword, and with blasting, and with mildew; and they shall pursue thee until thou perish.

The Lord will smite thee with the botch of Egypt, and with

the emerods, and with the scab, and with the itch, whereof thou canst not be healed. The Lord shall smite thee with madness, and blindness, and astonishment of heart.

The Lord shall smite thee in the knees, and in the legs, with a sore botch that cannot be healed, from the sole of thy foot unto the top of thy head.

If thou wilt not observe to do all the words of this law that are written in this book, that thou mayest fear this glorious and fearful name, THE LORD THY GOD; Then the Lord will make thy plagues wonderful, and the plagues of thy seed, even great plagues, and of long continuance, and sore sicknesses, and of long continuance. Moreover he will bring upon thee all the diseases of Egypt, which thou wast afraid of; and they shall cleave unto thee. Also every sickness, and every plague, which is not written in the book of this law, them will the Lord bring upon thee, until thou be destroyed.

Amp—But if you will not obey the voice of the Lord your God, being watchful to do all His commandments and His statutes which I command you this day, then all these curses shall come upon you and overtake you.

The Lord will smite you with consumption, with fever, and inflammation, fiery heat, sword and drought, blasting, and mildew; they shall pursue you until you perish.

The Lord will smite you with the boils of Egypt and the tumors, the scurvy and the itch, of which you cannot be healed. The Lord will smite you with madness and blindness and dismay of [mind and] heart.

The Lord will smite you on the knees and on the legs with a sore boil that cannot be healed, from the sole of your foot to the top of your head.

If you will not be watchful to do all the words of this law that are written in this book, that you may (reverently) fear this glorious and fearful name [and presence], THE LORD YOUR GOD; Then the Lord will bring upon you and your descendants extraordinary strokes and blows, great plagues of long continuance, and grievous sicknesses of long duration. Moreover He will bring upon you all the diseases of Egypt, of which you were afraid, and they shall cling to you. Also every sickness and every affliction which is not written in the book of this law, the Lord will bring upon you, until you are destroyed.

Moffatt—But if you will not listen to the voice of the Eternal your God, if you will not be mindful to carry out all his commands and rules which I enjoin upon you this day, then shall all these curses come upon you and overtake you.

The Eternal will strike you with consumption, fever, ague, and erysipelas, with drought, blasting, and mildew, that shall pursue you till you perish.

The Eternal will strike you with Egyptian boils, with tumours, scurvy, and itch incurable;

And the Eternal will strike your knees and legs with evil boils, incurable boils from head to foot. The Eternal will strike your minds with madness, blindness, and dismay, till you grope at noon like a blind man in the dark, and fall into disaster; you shall be utterly crushed and robbed continually, with no one to rescue you.

If you will not be mindful to carry out all the injunctions of this code written down in this book, revering the glorious and awful name of the Eternal your God, then the Eternal will inflict on you and your descendants amazing plagues, severe plagues and prolonged, diseases sore and prolonged; he will bring back upon you the diseases of Egypt that you were once afraid of, till they cleave to you; and the Eternal will also bring upon you any sickness and plague that is not mentioned in this book of the law, till you are ruined.

NEB—But if you do not obey the Lord your God by diligently observing all his commandments and statutes which I lay upon you this day, then all these maledictions shall come to you and light upon you.

May the Lord afflict you with wasting disease and recurrent fever, ague and eruptions; with drought, black blight and red; and may these plague you until you perish.

May the Lord strike you with Egyptian boils and with tumours, scabs, and itches, for which you will find no cure. May the Lord strike you with madness, blindness, and bewilderment.

May the Lord strike you on knee and leg with malignant boils for which you will find no cure; they will spread from the sole of your foot to the crown of your head.

If you do not observe and fulfil all the law written down in this book, if you do not revere this honoured and dreaded name, this name 'the Lord your God', then the Lord will strike you and your descendants with unimaginable plagues, malignant and persistent, and with sickness, persistent and severe. He will bring upon you once again all the diseases of Egypt which you dread, and they will cling to you. The Lord will bring upon you sickness and plague of every kind not written down in this book of the law, until you are destroyed.

Galatians 3:13-14, 29

KJV—Christ hath redeemed us from the curse of the law, being made a curse for us: for it is written, Cursed is every one that hangeth on a tree: That the blessing of Abraham might come on the Gentiles through Jesus Christ; that we might receive the promise of the Spirit through faith...And if ye be Christ's, then are ye Abraham's seed, and heirs according to the promise.

Amp—Christ purchased our freedom (redeeming us) from

the curse (doom) of the Law's (condemnation), by [Himself] becoming a curse for us, for it is written [in the Scriptures], Cursed is everyone who hangs on a tree (is crucified); To the end that through [their receiving] Christ Jesus, the blessing [promised] to Abraham might come upon the Gentiles, so that we through faith might [all] receive [the realization of] the promise of the (Holy) Spirit.

And if you belong to Christ (are in Him, Who is Abraham's Seed), then you are Abraham's offspring and (spiritual) heirs according to promise.

Moffatt—Christ ransomed us from the curse of the Law by becoming accursed for us (for it is written, Cursed is everyone who hangs on a gibbet), that the blessing of Abraham might reach the Gentiles in Christ Jesus, so that by faith we might receive the promised Spirit. Now if you are Christ's, then you are Abraham's offspring.

NEB—Christ bought us freedom from the curse of the law by becoming for our sake an accursed thing; for Scripture says, 'A curse is on everyone who is hanged on a gibbet.' And the purpose of it all was that the blessing of Abraham should in Jesus Christ be extended to the Gentiles, so that we might receive the promised Spirit through faith. But if you thus belong to Christ, you are the 'issue' of Abraham, and so heirs by promise.

Romans 8:2, 11

KJV—For the law of the Spirit of life in Christ Jesus hath made me free from the law of sin and death...But if the Spirit of him that raised up Jesus from the dead dwell in you, he that raised up Christ from the dead shall also quicken your mortal bodies by his Spirit that dwelleth in you.

Amp—For the law of the Spirit of life [which is] in Christ Jesus [the law of our new being], has freed me from the law of sin and of death. And if the Spirit of Him Who raised up Jesus from the dead dwells in you, [then] He Who raised up Christ Jesus from the dead will also restore to life your mortal (short-lived, perishable) bodies through His Spirit Who dwells in you.

Moffatt—The Law of the Spirit brings the life which is in Christ Jesus, and that law has set me free from the law of sin and death. And if the Spirit of Him who raised Jesus from the dead dwells within you, then He who raised Christ from the dead will also make your mortal bodies live by his indwelling Spirit in your lives.

NEB—Because in Christ Jesus the life-giving law of the Spirit has set you free from the law of sin and death. Moreover, if the Spirit of him who raised Jesus from the dead dwells within you, then the God who raised Christ Jesus from the dead will also give new life to your mortal bodies through his indwelling Spirit.

Colossians 1:13-14

KJV—Who hath delivered us from the power of darkness, and hath translated us into the kingdom of his dear Son: In whom we have redemption through his blood, even the forgiveness of sins.

Amp—[The Father] has delivered and drawn us to Himself out of the control and the dominion of darkness and has transferred us into the kingdom of the Son of His love, In Whom we have our redemption through His blood, [which means] the forgiveness of our sins.

Moffatt—Rescuing us from the power of the Darkness and transferring us to the realm of his beloved Son! In him we enjoy our redemption, that is, the forgiveness of sins.

NEB—He rescued us from the domain of darkness and brought us away into the kingdom of his dear Son, in whom our release is secured and our sins forgiven.

NAS—For (God) delivered us from the domain of darkness, and transferred us to the kingdom of His beloved Son, in whom we have redemption, the forgiveness of sins.

Colossians 2:13-15

KJV—And you, being dead in your sins and the uncircumcision of your flesh, hath he quickened together with him, having forgiven you all trespasses; Blotting out the handwriting of ordinances that was against us, which was contrary to us, and took it out of the way, nailing it to his cross; And having spoiled principalities and powers, he made a show of them openly, triumphing over them in it.

Amp—And you, who were dead in trespasses and in the uncircumcision of your flesh—your sensuality, your sinful carnal nature—[God] brought to life together with [Christ], having (freely) forgiven us all our transgressions; Having cancelled and blotted out and wiped away the handwriting of the note (or bond) with its legal decrees and demands, which was in force and stood against us—hostile to us. This [note with its regulations, decrees and demands] He set aside and cleared completely out of our way by nailing it to [His] cross. [God] disarmed the principalities and powers ranged against us and made a bold display and public example of them, in triumphing over them in Him and in it [the cross].

Moffatt—For though you were dead in your trespasses, your flesh uncircumcised, He made you live with Christ, He forgave us all our trespasses, He cancelled the regulations that stood against us—all these obligations he set aside when he nailed them to the cross, when he cut away the angelic Rulers and Powers from us, exposing them to all the world and triumphing over them in the cross.

NEB—And although you were dead because of your sins and because you were morally uncircumcised, he has made you alive with Christ. For he has forgiven us all our sins; he has cancelled the bond which pledged us to the decrees of the law. It stood against us, but he has set it aside, nailing it to the cross. On that cross he discarded the cosmic powers and authorities like a garment; he made a public spectacle of them and led them as captives in his triumphal procession.

1 John 3:8

KJV—For this purpose the Son of God was manifested, that he might destroy the works of the devil.

Amp—The reason the Son of God was made manifest (visible) was to undo (destroy, loosen and dissolve) the works the devil [has done].

Moffatt—He who commits sin belongs to the devil, for the devil is a sinner from the very beginning. (This is why the Son of God appeared, to destroy the deeds of the devil.)

NEB—The man who sins is a child of the devil, for the devil has been a sinner from the first; and the Son of God appeared for the very purpose of undoing the devil's work.

Revelation 12:11

KJV—And they overcame him by the blood of the Lamb, and by the word of their testimony; and they loved not their lives unto the death.

Amp—And they have overcome (conquered) him by means of the blood of the Lamb and by the utterance of their testimony, for they did not love and cling to life even when faced with death—holding their lives cheap till they had to die [for their witnessing].

Moffatt—But they have conquered him by the blood of the Lamb and by the word of their testimony; they had to die for it, but they did not cling to life.

NEB—By the sacrifice of the Lamb they have conquered him, and by the testimony which they uttered; for they did not hold their lives too dear to lay them down.

Healing in Redemption

* * *

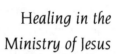

3

Healing in the
Ministry of Jesus

God has always provided
healing for His people.
Jesus revealed God's
will as He continually
ministered healing and
deliverance during His
time on earth. That has
not changed. He is still
the Healer!

Hebrews 13:8

KJV—Jesus Christ the same yesterday, and today, and for ever.

Amp—Jesus Christ, the Messiah, [is always] the same, yesterday, today, [yes,] and forever—to the ages.

Moffatt—Jesus Christ is always the same, yesterday, today, and for ever.

NEB—Jesus Christ is the same yesterday, today, and for ever.

Matthew 4:23-24

KJV—And Jesus went about all Galilee, teaching in their synagogues, and preaching the gospel of the kingdom, and healing all manner of sickness and all manner of disease among the people. And his fame went throughout all Syria: and they brought unto him all sick people that were taken with divers diseases and torments, and those which were possessed with devils, and those which were lunatic, and those that had the palsy and he healed them.

Amp—And He went about all Galilee, teaching in their synagogues and preaching the good news (Gospel) of the kingdom and healing every disease and every weakness and infirmity among the people. So the report of Him spread throughout all Syria, and they brought Him all that were sick, those afflicted with various diseases and torments, those under the power of demons, and epileptics, and paralyzed people; and He healed them.

Moffatt—Then he made a tour through the whole of Galilee, teaching in their synagogues, preaching the gospel of the Reign, and healing all sickness and disease among the people. The fame of him spread all through the surrounding country, and people brought him all their sick, those who suffered from all manner of disease and pain, demoniacs, epileptics, and paralytics; he healed them all.

NEB—He went round the whole of Galilee, teaching in the synagogues, preaching the gospel of the Kingdom, and curing whatever illness or infirmity there was among the people. His fame reached the whole of Syria; and sufferers from every kind of illness, racked with pain, possessed by devils, epileptic, or paralyzed, were all brought to him, and he cured them.

Matthew 8:2-3

KJV—And, behold, there came a leper and worshipped him, saying, Lord, if thou wilt, thou canst make me clean. And Jesus put forth his hand, and touched him, saying, I will; be thou clean. And immediately his leprosy was cleansed.

Amp—And behold, a leper came up to Him and prostrating himself, worshipped Him, saying, Lord, if You will, You are able to cleanse me by curing me. And He reached out His hand and touched him, saying, I will; be cleansed by being cured. And instantly his leprosy was cured and cleansed.

Moffatt—Up came a leper and knelt before him, saying, "If you only choose, sir, you can cleanse me"; so he stretched his hand out and touched him, with the words, "I do choose, be cleansed." And his leprosy was cleansed at once.

NEB—And now a leper approached him, bowed low, and said, 'Sir, if only you will, you can cleanse me.' Jesus stretched out his hand, touched him, and said, 'Indeed I will; be clean again.' And his leprosy was cured immediately.

Matthew 8:5-10, 13

KJV—And when Jesus was entered into Capernaum, there came unto him a centurion, beseeching him, And saying,

Lord, my servant lieth at home sick of the palsy, grievously tormented. And Jesus saith unto him, I will come and heal him. The centurion answered and said, Lord, I am not worthy that thou shouldest come under my roof: but speak the word only, and my servant shall be healed. For I am a man under authority, having soldiers under me: and I say to this man, Go, and he goeth; and to another, Come, and he cometh; and to my servant, Do this, and he doeth it.

When Jesus heard it, he marveled, and said to them that followed, Verily I say unto you, I have not found so great faith, no, not in Israel.

And Jesus said unto the centurion, Go thy way; and as thou hast believed, so be it done unto thee. And his servant was healed in the selfsame hour.

Amp—As Jesus went into Capernaum, a centurion came up to Him, begging Him And saying, Lord, my servant boy is lying at the house paralyzed and distressed with intense pains. And Jesus said to him, I will come and restore him. But the centurion replied to Him, Lord, I am not worthy or fit to have You come under my roof; but only speak the word, and my servant boy will be cured. For I also am a man subject to authority, with soldiers subject to me; and I say to one, Go, and he goes; and to another, Come, and he comes; and to my slave, Do this, and he does it. When Jesus heard him, He marveled, and said to those who followed Him [that is, who adhered steadfastly to Him, conforming to His example in living and if need be in dying also], I tell you, truly I have not found so much faith as this with any one, even in Israel.

Then to the centurion Jesus said, Go; it shall be done for you as you have believed. And the servant boy was restored to health at that very moment.

Moffatt—When he entered Capharnahum, an army-captain

came up to him and appealed to him, saying, "Sir, my servant is lying ill at home with paralysis, in terrible agony." He replied, "I will come and heal him." The captain answered, "Sir, I am not fit to have you under my roof; only say the word, and my servant will be cured. For though I am a man under authority myself, I have soldiers under me; I tell one man to go, and he goes, I tell another to come, and he comes, I tell my servant, 'Do this,' and he does it."

When Jesus heard that, he marvelled; "I tell you truly," he said to his followers, "I have never met faith like this anywhere in Israel."

Then said Jesus to the captain, "Go; as you have had faith, your prayer is granted." And the servant was cured at that very hour.

NEB—When he had entered Capernaum a centurion came up to ask his help. 'Sir,' he said, 'a boy of mine lies at home paralysed and racked with pain.' Jesus said, 'I will come and cure him.' But the centurion replied, 'Sir, who am I to have you under my roof? You need only say the word and the boy will be cured. I know, for I am myself under orders, with soldiers under me. I say to one, "Go", and he goes; to another, "Come here", and he comes; and to my servant, "Do this", and he does it.'

Jesus heard him with astonishment, and said to the people who were following him, 'I tell you this: nowhere, even in Israel, have I found such faith.'

Then Jesus said to the centurion, 'Go home now; because of your faith, so let it be.' At that moment the boy recovered.

Matthew 8:16-17

KJV—When the even was come, they brought unto him many that were possessed with devils: and he cast out the spirits with his word, and healed all that were sick: That it might be fulfilled which was spoken by Esaias the prophet, saying, Himself took our infirmities and bare our sicknesses.

Amp—When evening came they brought to Him many who were under the power of demons, and He drove out the spirits with a word, and restored to health all who were sick; And thus He fulfilled what was spoken by the prophet Isaiah, He Himself took (in order to carry away) our weaknesses and infirmities and bore away our diseases.

Moffatt—Now when evening came they brought him many demoniacs, and he cast out the spirits with a word and healed all the invalids—that the word spoken by the prophet Isaiah might be fulfilled, He took away our sicknesses and our diseases he removed.

NEB—When evening fell, they brought to him many who were possessed by devils; and he drove the spirits out with a word and healed all who were sick, to fulfil the prophecy of Isaiah: 'He took away our illnesses and lifted our diseases from us.'

Matthew 9:18-29

KJV—While he spake these things unto them, behold, there came a certain ruler, and worshipped him, saying, My daughter is even now dead: but come and lay thy hand upon her and she shall live. And Jesus arose, and followed him, and so did his disciples.

And, behold, a woman, which was diseased with an issue of blood twelve years, came behind him, and touched the hem of his garment: For she said within herself, If I may but touch his garment, I shall be whole. But Jesus turned him about, and when he saw her, he said, Daughter, be of good comfort; thy faith hath made thee whole. And the woman was made whole from that hour.

And when Jesus came into the ruler's house, and saw the minstrels and the people making a noise, He said unto them, Give place: for the maid is not dead, but sleepeth. And they laughed him to scorn. But when the people were put forth, he went in, and took her by the hand, and the maid arose. And the fame hereof went abroad into all that land.

And when Jesus departed thence, two blind men followed him, crying, and saying, Thou son of David, have mercy on us. And when he was come into the house, the blind men came to him: and Jesus saith unto them, Believe ye that I am able to do this? They said unto him, Yea, Lord. Then touched he their eyes, saying, According to your faith be it unto you.

Amp—While He was talking this way to them, behold, a ruler entered and kneeling down, worshipped Him, saying, My daughter has just now died; but come and lay Your hand on her and she will come to life. And Jesus got up and accompanied him, with His disciples.

And behold, a woman who had suffered from a flow of blood for twelve years came up behind Him and touched the fringe of His garment; For she kept saying to herself, If I only touch His garment, I shall be restored to health. Jesus turned around and seeing her He said, Take courage, daughter! Your faith has made you well. And at once the woman was restored to health.

And when Jesus came to the ruler's house and saw the flute players, and the crowd making an uproar and din, He said, Go away; for the girl is not dead but sleeping. And they laughed and jeered at Him. But when the crowd had been ordered to go outside, He went in and took her by the hand, and the girl arose. And the news about this spread through all that district.

As Jesus was passing on from there, two blind men followed Him, shouting loudly, Have pity and mercy on us, Son of David! When He reached the house and went in, the blind men came to Him. And Jesus said to them, Do you believe that I am able to do this? They said to Him, Yes, Lord. Then He touched their eyes, saying, According to your faith and trust and reliance [on the power invested in Me] be it done to you.

Moffatt—As he said this, an official came in and knelt before him, saying, "My daughter is just dead; do come and lay your hands on her, and she will live." So Jesus rose and went after him, accompanied by his disciples.

A woman who had had a hemorrhage for twelve years came up behind him and touched the tassel of his robe; what she said to herself was this, "If I can only touch his robe, I will recover." Then Jesus turned round, and when he saw her he said, "Courage, my daughter, your faith has made you well." And instantly the woman was well.

Now when Jesus reached the official's house and saw the flute-players and the din the crowd were making, he said, "Begone; the girl is not dead but asleep." They laughed at him. But after the crowd had been put out, he went in and took her hand, and the girl rose up. The report of this went all over that country.

As Jesus passed along from there, he was followed by two blind men who shrieked, "Son of David, have pity on us!" When he went indoors, the blind men came up to him, and Jesus asked them, "Do you believe I can do this?" They said, "Yes, sir." Then he touched their eyes, saying, "As you believe, so your prayer is granted."

NEB—Even as he spoke, there came a president of the synagogue, who bowed low before him and said, 'My daughter has just died; but come and lay your hand on her, and she will live.' Jesus rose and went with him, and so did his disciples.

Then a woman who had suffered from haemorrhages for twelve years came up from behind, and touched the edge of his cloak; for she said to herself, 'If I can only touch his cloak, I shall be cured.' But Jesus turned and saw her, and said, 'Take heart, my daughter; your faith has cured you.' And from that moment she recovered.

When Jesus arrived at the president's house and saw the flute-players and the general commotion, he said, 'Be off! The girl is not dead: she is asleep'; and they only laughed at him. But, when everyone had been turned out, he went into the room and took the girl by the hand, and she got up. This story became the talk of all the country round.

As he passed on Jesus was followed by two blind men, who cried out, 'Son of David, have pity on us!' And when he had gone indoors they came to him. Jesus asked, 'Do you believe that I have the power to do what you want?' 'Yes, sir', they said. Then he touched their eyes, and said, 'As you have believed, so let it be'.

Matthew 9:35

KJV—And Jesus went about all the cities and villages, teaching in their synagogues, and preaching the gospel of the kingdom, and healing every sickness and every disease among the people.

Amp—And Jesus went about all the cities and villages, teaching in their synagogues and proclaiming the good news (the Gospel) of the kingdom, and curing all kinds of disease and every weakness and infirmity.

Moffatt—Then Jesus made a tour through all the towns and villages, teaching in their synagogues, preaching the gospel of the Reign, and healing every sickness and disease.

NEB—So Jesus went round all the towns and villages teaching in their synagogues, announcing the good news of the Kingdom, and curing every kind of ailment and disease.

Matthew 12:9-13

KJV—And when he was departed thence, he went into their synagogue: And, behold, there was a man which had his hand withered. And they asked him, saying, Is it lawful to heal on the sabbath days? that they might accuse him. And he said unto them, What man shall there be among you, that shall have one sheep, and if it fall into a pit on the sabbath day, will he not lay hold on it, and lift it out? How much then is a man better than a sheep? Wherefore it is lawful to do well on the sabbath days. Then saith he to the man, Stretch forth thine hand. And he stretched it forth; and it was restored whole, like as the other.

Amp—And going on from there, He went into their synagogue. And behold, a man was there with one withered hand. And they said to Him, Is it lawful or allowable to cure people on the Sabbath days? that they might accuse him. But He said to them, What man is there among you, if he has only one sheep, and it falls into a pit or ditch on the Sabbath, will not take hold of it and lift it out? How much better and of more value is a man than a sheep! So it is lawful and allowable to do good on the Sabbath days. Then He said to the man, Reach out your hand. And the man reached it out, and it was restored, sound as the other one.

Moffatt—Then he moved on from there and went into their synagogue. Now a man with a withered hand was there; so in order to get a charge against him, they asked him, "Is it right to heal on the sabbath?" He said to them, "Is there a man of you with one sheep, who will not catch hold of it and lift it out of a pit on the sabbath, if it falls in? And how much more is a man worth than a sheep? Thus it is right to do a kindness on the sabbath." Then he said to the man, "Stretch out your hand." He stretched it out, and it was restored, as sound as the other.

NEB—He went on to another place, and entered their synagogue. A man was there with a withered arm, and they asked Jesus, 'Is it permitted to heal on the Sabbath?' (They wanted to frame a charge against him.) But he said to them, 'Suppose you had one sheep, which fell into a ditch on the Sabbath; is there one of you who would not catch hold of it and lift it out? And surely a man is worth far more than a sheep! It is therefore permitted to do good on the Sabbath.' Turning to the man he said, 'Stretch out your arm.' He stretched it out, and it was made sound again like the other.

Matthew 12:22

KJV—Then was brought unto him one possessed with a devil, blind, and dumb: and he healed him, insomuch that the blind and dumb both spake and saw.

Amp—Then a blind and dumb man, under the power of a demon, was brought to Jesus, and He cured him, so that the blind and dumb man both spoke and saw.

Moffatt—Then a blind and dumb demoniac was brought to him, and he healed him, so that the dumb man spoke and saw.

NEB—Then they brought him a man who was possessed; he was blind and dumb; and Jesus cured him, restoring both speech and sight.

Matthew 14:14

KJV—And Jesus went forth, and saw a great multitude, and was moved with compassion toward them, and he healed their sick.

Amp—When He went ashore and saw a great throng of people, He had compassion (pity and deep sympathy) for them and cured their sick.

Moffatt—So when he disembarked, he saw a large crowd, and out of pity for them he healed their sick folk.

NEB—When he came ashore, he saw a great crowd; his heart went out to them, and he cured those of them who were sick.

Matthew 14:34-36

KJV—And when (Jesus and His disciples) were gone over, they came into the land of Gennesaret. And when the men of that place had knowledge of him, they sent out into all that country round about, and brought unto him all that were diseased; And besought him that they might only touch the hem of his garment: and as many as touched were made perfectly whole.

Amp—And when they had crossed over to the other side, they went ashore at Gennesaret. And when the men of that place recognized Him, they sent around into all the surrounding country and brought to Him all that were sick, And begged Him to let them merely touch the fringe of His garment; and as many as touched it were perfectly restored.

Moffatt—On crossing over they came to land at Gennesaret. The men of that place recognized him and sent all over the surrounding country, bringing him all who were ill and begging him to let them touch the mere tassel of his robe—and all who touched it got perfectly well.

NEB—So they finished the crossing and came to land at Gennesaret. There Jesus was recognized by the people of the place, who sent out word to all the country round. And all who were ill were brought to him, and he was begged to allow them simply to touch the edge of his cloak. And everyone who touched it was completely cured.

Matthew 15:30-31

KJV—And great multitudes came unto him, having with them those that were lame, blind, dumb, maimed, and many others, and cast them down at Jesus' feet; and he healed them: Insomuch that the multitude wondered, when they saw the dumb to speak, the maimed to be whole, the lame to walk, and the blind to see: and they glorified the God of Israel.

Amp—And a great multitude came to Him, bringing with them the lame, the maimed, the blind, the dumb, and many others, and they put them down at His feet and He cured them. So that the crowd was amazed when they saw the dumb speaking, the maimed whole, the lame walking, and the blind seeing, and they recognized and praised and thanked and glorified the God of Israel.

Moffatt—And large crowds came to him bringing the lame and the blind, the dumb, the maimed, and many others; they laid them at his feet, and he healed them. This made the crowd wonder, to see dumb people speaking, the lame walking, and the blind seeing. And they glorified the God of Israel.

NEB—When he was seated there, crowds flocked to him, bringing with them the lame, blind, dumb, and crippled, and many other sufferers; they threw them down at his feet, and he healed them. Great was the amazement of the people when they saw the dumb speaking, the crippled strong, the lame walking, and sight restored to the blind; and they gave praise to the God of Israel.

Matthew 20:29-34

KJV—And as they departed from Jericho, a great multitude followed him. And, behold, two blind men sitting by the way side, when they heard that Jesus passed by, cried out, saying, Have mercy on us, O Lord, thou Son of David. And the multitude rebuked them, because they should hold their peace: but they cried the more, saying, Have mercy on us, O Lord, thou Son of David. And Jesus stood still, and called them, and said, What will ye that I shall do unto you? They say unto him, Lord, that our eyes may be opened. So Jesus had compassion on them, and touched their eyes: and immediately their eyes received sight, and they followed him.

Amp—And as they were going out of Jericho, a great throng accompanied Him. And behold, two blind men were sitting by the roadside, and when they heard that Jesus was passing by, they cried out, Lord, have pity and mercy on us, [You] Son of David! The crowds reproved them and told them to keep still; but they cried out the more, Lord, have pity and mercy on us, [You] Son of David! And Jesus stopped and called them, and asked, What do you want Me to do for you? They answered Him, Lord, we want our eyes to be opened! And Jesus in pity touched their eyes, and instantly they received their sight and followed Him.

Moffatt—As they were leaving Jericho, a crowd followed him, and when two blind men who were sitting beside the road heard Jesus was passing, they shouted, "O Lord, Son of David, have pity on us!" The crowd checked them and told them to be quiet, but they shouted all the louder, "O Lord, Son of David, have pity on us!" So Jesus stopped and called them. He said, "What do you want me to do for you?" "Lord," they said, "we want our eyes opened." Then Jesus in pity touched their eyes, and they regained their sight at once and followed him.

NEB—As they were leaving Jericho he was followed by a great crowd of people. At the roadside sat two blind men. When they heard it said that Jesus was passing they shouted, 'Have pity on us, Son of David.' The people told them sharply to be quiet. But they shouted all the more, 'Sir, have pity on us, have pity on us; Son of David.' Jesus stopped and called the men. 'What do you want me to do for you?' he asked. 'Sir,' they answered, 'we want our sight.' Jesus was deeply moved, and touched their eyes. At once their sight came back, and they followed him.

Matthew 21:14

KJV—And the blind and the lame came to him in the temple; and he healed them.

Amp—And the blind and the lame came to Him in the porches and courts of the temple, and He cured them.

Moffatt—Blind and lame people came up to him in the temple, and he healed them.

NEB—In the temple blind men and cripples came to him, and he healed them.

Mark 1:40-42

KJV—And there came a leper to him, beseeching him, and kneeling down to him, and saying unto him, If thou wilt, thou canst make me clean. And Jesus, moved with compassion, put forth his hand, and touched him, and saith unto him, I will; be thou clean. And, as soon as he had spoken, immediately the leprosy departed from him, and he was cleansed.

Amp—And a leper came to Him, begging Him on his knees and saying to Him, If You will, You are able to make me clean. And being moved with pity and sympathy, Jesus reached out His hand and touched him, and said to him, I will; be made clean! And at once the leprosy [completely] left him, and he was made clean (by being healed).

Moffatt—A leper came to him, beseeching him on bended knee, saying, "If you only choose, you can cleanse me"; so he stretched his hand out in pity and touched him saying, "I do choose, be cleansed." As he spoke, the leprosy at once left the man, and he was cleansed.

NEB—Once he was approached by a leper, who knelt before

him begging his help. 'If only you will,' said the man, 'you can cleanse me.' In warm indignation Jesus stretched out his hand, touched him, and said, 'Indeed I will; be clean again.' The leprosy left him immediately, and he was clean.

Mark 5:21-42

KJV—And when Jesus was passed over again by ship unto the other side, much people gathered unto him: and he was nigh unto the sea. And, behold, there cometh one of the rulers of the synagogue, Jairus by name; and when he saw him, he fell at his feet, And besought him greatly, saying, My little daughter lieth at the point of death: I pray thee, come and lay thy hands on her, that she may be healed; and she shall live. And Jesus went with him; and much people followed him, and thronged him.

And a certain woman, which had an issue of blood twelve years, And had suffered many things of many physicians, and had spent all that she had, and was nothing bettered, but rather grew worse, When she had heard of Jesus, came in the press behind, and touched his garment. For she said, If I may touch but his clothes, I shall be whole. And straightway the fountain of her blood was dried up; and she felt in her body that she was healed of that plague.

And Jesus, immediately knowing in himself that virtue had gone out of him, turned him about in the press, and said, Who touched my clothes? And his disciples said unto him, Thou seest the multitude thronging thee, and sayest thou, Who touched me? And he looked round about to see her that had done this thing. But the woman fearing and trembling, knowing what was done in her, came and fell down before him, and told him all the truth. And he said unto her, Daughter, thy faith hath made thee whole; go in peace, and be whole of thy plague.

While he yet spake, there came from the ruler of the

synagogue's house certain which said, Thy daughter is dead: why troublest thou the Master any further? As soon as Jesus heard the word that was spoken, he saith unto the ruler of the synagogue, Be not afraid, only believe. And he suffered no man to follow him, save Peter, and James, and John the brother of James. And he cometh to the house of the ruler of the synagogue, and seeth the tumult, and them that wept and wailed greatly. And when he was come in, he saith unto them, Why make ye this ado, and weep? the damsel is not dead, but sleepeth.

And they laughed him to scorn. But when he had put them all out, he taketh the father and the mother of the damsel, and them that were with him, and entereth in where the damsel was lying. And he took the damsel by the hand, and said unto her, Talitha cumi; which is, being interpreted, Damsel, I say unto thee, arise. And straightway the damsel arose, and walked; for she was of the age of twelve years. And they were astonished with a great astonishment.

Amp—And when Jesus had recrossed in the boat to the other side, a great throng gathered about Him, and He was at the lakeshore. Then one of the rulers of the synagogue came up, Jairus by name; and seeing Him, he prostrated himself at His feet, and begged Him earnestly, saying, My little daughter is at the point of death. Come and lay Your hands on her, so that she may be healed and live. And Jesus went with him, and a great crowd kept following Him, and pressed Him from all sides—so as almost to suffocate Him.

And there was a woman who had had a flow of blood for twelve years, And who had endured much suffering under [the hands of] many physicians, and had spent all that she had; and was no better but instead grew worse. She had heard the reports concerning Jesus, and she came up behind Him in the throng and touched His garment, For she kept saying, If I only touch His garments, I shall be restored to health. And immediately her (flow of) blood was dried up at the source, and (suddenly) she felt in her body that she was healed of her (distressing) ailment.

And Jesus, recognizing in Himself that the power proceeding from Him had gone forth, turned around immediately in the crowd, and said, Who touched My clothes? And the disciples kept saying to Him, You see the crowd pressing hard around You (from all sides), and You ask, Who touched Me? Still He kept looking around to see her who had done it. But the woman, knowing what had been done for her, though alarmed and frightened and trembling, fell down before Him, and told Him the whole truth. And He said to her, Daughter, your faith [that is, your trust and confidence in Me, springing from faith in God] has restored you to health. Go in (to) peace, and be continually healed and free from your (distressing bodily) disease.

While He was still speaking, there came some from the ruler's house who said [to Jairus], Your daughter has died. Why bother and distress the Teacher any further? (Overhearing) but ignoring what they said, Jesus said to the ruler of the synagogue, Do not be seized with alarm and have no fear, only keep on believing. And He permitted no one to accompany Him except Peter and James and John the brother of James. When they arrived at the house of the ruler of the synagogue, He looked (carefully and with understanding) at [the] tumult and [the people] weeping and wailing loudly. And when He had gone in, He said to them, Why do you make an uproar and weep? The little girl is not dead, but is sleeping.

And they laughed and jeered at Him. But He put them all out, and taking the child's father and mother and those who were with Him, He went in where the little girl was lying. Gripping her (firmly) by the hand, He said to her, Talitha cumi, which translated is, Little girl, I say to you, arise (from the sleep of death)! And instantly the girl got up and started walking around, for she was twelve years [old]. And they were utterly astonished and overcome with amazement.

Moffatt—Now when Jesus had crossed back in the boat to the other side, a large crowd gathered round him; so he remained beside the sea. A president of the synagogue, called Jairus, came up, and on catching sight of him fell at his feet with earnest entreaties. "My little girl is dying," he said, "do come and lay your hands on her, that she may recover and live." So Jesus went away with him. Now a large crowd followed him; they pressed round him.

And there was a woman who had a hemorrhage for twelve years—she had suffered much under a number of doctors, and had spent all her means, but was none the better; in fact she was rather worse. Hearing about Jesus, she got behind him in the crowd, and touched his robe; "if I can touch even his clothes," she said to herself, "I will recover." And at once the hemorrhage stopped; she felt in her body that she was cured of her complaint.

Healing in the Ministry of Jesus

Jesus was at once conscious that some healing virtue had passed from him, so he turned round in the crowd and asked, "Who touched my clothes?" His disciples said to him, "You see the crowd are pressing round you, and yet you ask, 'Who touched me?'" But he kept looking round to see who had done it, and the woman, knowing what had happened to her, came forward in fear and trembling and fell down before him, telling him all the truth. "Daughter," he said to her, "your faith has made you well; go in peace and be free from your complaint."

He was still speaking when a message came from the house of the synagogue-president, "Your daughter is dead. Why trouble the teacher to come any further?" Instantly Jesus ignored the remark and told the president, "Have no fear, only believe." He would not allow any to accompany him, except Peter and James and John the brother of James. So they reached the president's house, where he saw a tumult of people wailing and making shrill lament; and on entering he asked them, "Why make a noise and wail? The child is not dead but asleep."

They laughed at him. However, he put them all outside and taking the father and mother of the child as well as his companions he went in to where the child was lying; then he took the child's hand and said to her, "Talitha koum"—which may be translated, "Little girl, rise, I tell you." The girl got up at once and began to walk (she was twelve years old); and at once they were lost in utter amazement.

NEB—As soon as Jesus had returned by boat to the other shore, a great crowd once more gathered round him. While he was by the lake-side, the president of one of the synagogues came up, Jairus by name, and, when he saw him, threw himself down at his feet and pleaded with him. 'My little daughter', he said, 'is at death's door. I beg you to come and lay your hands on her to cure her and save her life.' So Jesus went with him, accompanied by a great crowd which pressed upon him.

Among them was a woman who had suffered from haemorrhages for twelve years; and in spite of long treatment by many doctors, on which she had spent all she had, there had been no improvement; on the contrary, she had grown worse. She had heard what people were saying about Jesus, so she came up from behind in the crowd and touched his cloak; for she said to herself, 'If I touch even his clothes, I shall be cured.' And there and then the source of her haemorrhages dried up and she knew in herself that she was cured of her trouble.

At the same time Jesus, aware that power had gone out of him, turned round in the crowd and asked, 'Who touched my clothes?' His disciples said to him, 'You see the crowd pressing upon you and yet you ask, "Who touched me?"' Meanwhile he was looking round to see who had done it. And the woman, trembling with fear when she grasped what had happened to her, came and fell at his feet and told him the whole truth. He said to her, 'My daughter, your faith has cured you. Go in peace, free for ever from this trouble.'

While he was still speaking, a message came from the president's house, 'Your daughter is dead; why trouble the Rabbi further?' But Jesus, overhearing the message as it was delivered, said to the president of the synagogue, 'Do not be afraid; only have faith.' After this he allowed no one to accompany him except Peter and James and James's brother John. They came to the president's house, where he found a great commotion, with loud crying and wailing. So he went in and said to them, 'Why this crying and commotion? The child is not dead: she is asleep';

And they only laughed at him. But after turning all the others out, he took the child's father and mother and his own companions and went in where the child was lying. Then, taking hold of her hand, he said to her, 'Talitha cum', which means, 'Get up, my child.' Immediately the girl got up and walked about—she was twelve years old. At that they were beside themselves with amazement.

Mark 6:53-56

KJV—And when (Jesus and his disciples) had passed over, they came into the land of Gennesaret, and drew to the shore. And when they were come out of the ship, straightway they knew him, And ran through that whole region round about, and began to carry about in beds those that were sick, where they heard he was. And whithersoever he entered, into villages, or cities, or country, they laid the sick in the streets, and besought him that they might touch if it were but the border of his garment: and as many as touched him were made whole.

Amp—And when they had crossed over they reached the land of Gennesaret, and came to (anchor at) the shore. As soon as they got out of the boat [the people] recognized Him, And they ran about the whole countryside, and began to carry around sick people on their pallets (sleeping pads) to any place where they heard that He was. And wherever He came into villages or cities or the country, they would lay the sick in the market places, and beg Him that they might touch even the fringe of His outer garment; and as many as touched Him were restored to health.

Moffatt—On crossing over, they came to land at Gennesaret and moored to the shore. And when they disembarked, the people at once recognized Jesus; they hurried round all the district and proceeded to carry the sick on their pallets, wherever they heard that he was; whatever village or town or hamlet he went to, they would lay their invalids in the marketplace, begging him to let them touch even the tassel of his robe—and all who touched him recovered.

NEB—So they finished the crossing and came to land at Gennesaret, where they made fast. When they came ashore, he was immediately recognized; and the people scoured that whole country-side and brought the sick on stretchers to any place where he was reported to be. Wherever he went, to farmsteads, villages, or towns, they laid out the sick in the market-places and begged him to let them simply touch the edge of his cloak; and all who touched him were cured.

Mark 7:31-37

KJV—And again, departing from the coasts of Tyre and Sidon, he came unto the sea of Galilee, through the midst of the coasts of Decapolis. And they bring unto him one that was deaf, and had an impediment in his speech; and they beseech him to put his hand upon him. And he took him aside from the multitude, and put his fingers into his ears, and he spit, and touched his tongue; And looking up to heaven, he sighed, and saith unto him, Ephphatha, that is, Be opened. And straightway his ears were opened, and the string of his tongue was loosed, and he spake plain.

And he charged them that they should tell no man: but the more he charged them, so much the more a great deal they published it; And were beyond measure astonished, saying, He hath done all things well: he maketh both the deaf to hear, and the dumb to speak.

Amp—Soon after this Jesus coming back from the region of Tyre, passed through Sidon on to the Sea of Galilee through the region of Decapolis [the ten cities]. And they brought to Him a man who was deaf and had difficulty in speaking, and they begged Jesus to place His hand upon him. And taking him aside from the crowd privately, He thrust His fingers into the man's ears, and spat and touched his tongue; And looking up to heaven, He sighed as He said, Ephphatha, which means, Be opened. And his ears were opened, his tongue was loosed, and he began to speak distinctly and as he should.

And Jesus [in His own interest] admonished and ordered them sternly and expressly to tell no one, but the more He commanded them, the more zealously they proclaimed it. And they were overwhelmingly astonished, saying, He has done everything excellently—commendably and nobly! He even makes the deaf to hear and the dumb to speak!

Moffatt—He left the territory of Tyre again and passed through Sidon to the sea of Galilee, crossing the territory of Decapolis. And a deaf man who stammered was brought to him, with the request that he would lay his hand on him. So, taking him aside from the crowd by himself, he put his fingers into the man's ears, touched his tongue with saliva, and looking up to heaven with a deep sigh he said to him, "Ephphatha" (which means, Open!). Then his ears were at once opened and his tongue freed from its fetter—he began to speak correctly.

Jesus forbade them to tell anyone about it, but the more he forbade them the more eagerly they made it public; they were astounded in the extreme, saying, "How splendidly he has done it all! He actually makes the deaf hear and the dumb speak!"

NEB—On his return journey from Tyrian territory he went by way of Sidon to the Sea of Galilee through the territory of the Ten Towns. They brought to him a man who was deaf and had an impediment in his speech, with the request that he would lay his hand on him. He took the man aside, away from the crowd, put his fingers into his ears, spat, and touched his tongue. Then, looking up to heaven, he sighed, and said to him, 'Ephphatha', which means 'Be opened.' With that his ears were opened, and at the same time the impediment was removed and he spoke plainly.

Jesus forbade them to tell anyone; but the more he forbade them, the more they published it. Their astonishment knew no bounds: 'All that he does, he does well,' they said; 'he even makes the deaf hear and the dumb speak.'

Mark 8:22-25

KJV—And (Jesus) cometh to Bethsaida; and they bring a blind man unto him, and besought him to touch him. And he took the blind man by the hand, and led him out of the town; and when he had spit on his eyes, and put his hands upon him, he asked him if he saw aught. And he looked up, and said, I see men as trees, walking. After that he put his hands again upon his eyes, and made him look up: and he was restored, and saw every man clearly.

Amp—And they came to Bethsaida. And [people] brought to Him a blind man, and begged Him to touch him. And He caught the blind man by the hand, and led him out of the village; and when He had spit on his eyes and put His hands upon him, He asked him, Do you (possibly) see anything? And he looked up and said, I see people, but [they look] like trees, walking. Then He put His hands on his eyes again, and the man looked intently [that is, fixed his eyes on definite objects], and he was restored, and saw everything distinctly—even what was at a distance.

Moffatt—Then they reached Bethsaida. A blind man was brought to him, with the request that he would touch him. So he took the blind man by the hand and led him outside the village; then, after spitting on his eyes, he laid his hands on him and asked him, "Do you see anything?" He began to see, and said, "I can make out people, for I see them as large as trees moving." At this he laid his hands once more on his eyes, and the man stared in front of him; he was quite restored, he saw everything distinctly.

NEB—They arrived at Bethsaida. There the people brought a blind man to Jesus and begged him to touch him. He took the blind man by the hand and led him away out of the village. Then he spat on his eyes, laid his hands upon him, and asked whether he could see anything. The man's sight began to come back, and he said, 'I see men; they look like trees, but they are walking about.' Jesus laid his hands on his eyes again; he looked hard, and now he was cured so that he saw everything clearly.

Luke 4:16-21

KJV—And (Jesus) came to Nazareth, where he had been brought up: and, as his custom was, he went into the synagogue on the sabbath day, and stood up for to read. And there was delivered unto him the book of the prophet Esaias. And when he had opened the book, he found the place where it was written,

The Spirit of the Lord is upon me, because he hath anointed me to preach the gospel to the poor; he hath sent me to heal the brokenhearted, to preach deliverance to the captives, and recovering of sight to the blind, to set at liberty them that are bruised, To preach the acceptable year of the Lord. And he closed the book, and he gave it again to the minister, and sat down. And the eyes of all them that were in the synagogue were fastened on him. And he began to say unto them, This day is this Scripture fulfilled in your ears.

Amp—So He came to Nazareth, [that Nazareth] where He had been brought up; and He entered the synagogue, as was His custom on the Sabbath day. And He stood up to read. And there was handed to Him [the roll of] the book of the prophet Isaiah. He opened (unrolled) the book, and found the place where it was written,

The Spirit of the Lord [is] upon Me, because He has anointed Me [the Anointed One, the Messiah] to preach the good news (the Gospel) to the poor; He has sent Me to announce release to the captives, and recovery of sight to the blind; to send forth delivered those who are oppressed—who are downtrodden, bruised, crushed and broken down by calamity; To proclaim the accepted and acceptable year of the Lord—the day when salvation and the free favors of God profusely abound. Then He rolled up the book, and gave it back to the attendant and sat down; and the eyes of all in the synagogue were gazing (attentively) at Him. And He began to speak to them: Today this Scripture has been fulfilled while you are present and hearing.

Moffatt—Coming to Nazaret, where he had been brought up, on the sabbath he entered the synagogue as was his custom. He stood up to read the lesson, and was handed the book of the prophet Isaiah; on opening the book he came upon the place where it was written,

The Spirit of the Lord is upon me: for he has consecrated me to preach the gospel to the poor, he has sent me to proclaim release for captives and recovery of sight for the blind, to set free the oppressed, to proclaim the Lord's year of favour. Then, folding up the book, he handed it back to the attendant and sat down. The eyes of all in the synagogue were fixed on him, and he proceeded to tell them that "To-day, this scripture is fulfilled in your hearing."

NEB—So he came to Nazareth, where he had been brought up, and went to synagogue on the Sabbath day as he regularly did. He stood up to read the lesson and was handed the scroll of the prophet Isaiah. He opened the scroll and found the passage which says,

'The spirit of the Lord is upon me because he has anointed me; he has sent me to announce good news to the poor, to proclaim release for prisoners and recovery of sight for the blind; to let the broken victims go free, to proclaim the year of the Lord's favour.' He rolled up the scroll, gave it back to the attendant, and sat down; and all eyes in the synagogue were fixed on him. He began to speak: 'Today', he said, 'in your very hearing this text has come true.'

Luke 4:40

KJV—Now when the sun was setting, all they that had any sick with divers diseases brought them unto him; and he laid his hands on every one of them, and healed them.

Amp—Now at the setting of the sun [indicating the end of the Sabbath], all those who had [any that were] sick with various diseases brought them to Him, and He laid His hands upon every one of them and cured them.

Moffatt—At sunset all who had any people ill with any sort of disease brought them to him: he laid his hands on everyone and healed them.

NEB—At sunset all who had friends suffering from one disease or another brought them to him; and he laid his hands on them one by one and cured them.

Luke 5:15

KJV—But so much the more went there a fame abroad of him: and great multitudes came together to hear, and to be healed by him of their infirmities.

Amp—But so much the more the news spread abroad concerning Him and great crowds kept coming together to hear and to be healed by Him of their infirmities.

Moffatt—But the news of him spread abroad more and more; large crowds gathered to hear him and to be healed of their complaints.

NEB—But the talk about him spread all the more; great crowds gathered to hear him and to be cured of their ailments.

Luke 5:17-25

KJV—And it came to pass on a certain day, as (Jesus) was teaching, that there were Pharisees and doctors of the law sitting by, which were come out of every town of Galilee, and Judea, and Jerusalem: and the power of the Lord was present to heal them.

And, behold, men brought in a bed a man which was taken with a palsy: and they sought means to bring him in, and to lay him before him. And when they could not find by what way they might bring him in because of the multitude, they went upon the housetop, and let him down through the tiling with his couch into the midst before Jesus.

And when he saw their faith, he said unto him, Man, thy sins are forgiven thee. And the scribes and the Pharisees began to reason, saying, Who is this which speaketh blasphemies? Who can forgive sins, but God alone? But when Jesus perceived their thoughts, he answering said unto them, What reason ye in your hearts? Whether is easier, to say, Thy sins be forgiven thee; or to say, Rise up and walk? But that ye may know that the Son of man hath power upon earth to forgive sins, (he said unto the sick of the palsy,) I say unto thee, Arise, and take up thy couch, and go into thine house. And immediately he rose up before them, and took up that whereon he lay, and departed to his own house, glorifying God.

Amp—One of those days, as He was teaching, there were Pharisees and teachers of the Law sitting by, who had come from every village and town of Galilee and Judea and from Jerusalem. And the power of the Lord was with Him (present) to heal (them).

And behold, some men were bringing on a stretcher a man who was paralyzed, and they tried to carry him in and lay him before [Jesus]. But finding no way to bring him in, because of the crowd, they went up on the roof, and lowered him with his stretcher down through the tiles into the midst in front of Jesus.

And when He saw [their confidence in Him, springing from] their faith, He said, Man, your sins are forgiven you! And the scribes and the Pharisees began to reason and question and argue, saying, Who is this [Man] Who speaks blasphemies? Who can forgive sins but God alone? But Jesus, knowing their thoughts and questionings, answered them, Why do you question in your hearts? Which is easier, to say, Your sins are forgiven you, or to say, Arise and walk (about)? But that you may know that the Son of man has the (power of) authority and right on earth to forgive sins, He said to the paralyzed man, I say to you, arise, pick up your litter (little bed), and go to your own house! And instantly the man stood up before them, and picked up what he had been lying on, and went away to his house, recognizing and praising and thanking God.

Moffatt—One day he was teaching, and near him sat Pharisees and doctors of the Law who had come from every village of Galilee and Judaea as well as from Jerusalem. Now the power of the Lord was present for the work of healing.

Some men came up, carrying a man who was paralysed; they tried to carry him inside and lay him in front of Jesus, but when they could not find any means of getting him in, on account of the crowd, they climbed to the top of the house and let him down through the tiles, mattress and all, among people in front of Jesus.

When he saw their faith, he said, "Man, your sins are forgiven you." Then the scribes and Pharisees began to argue, "Who is this blasphemer? Who can forgive sins, who but God alone?" Conscious that they were arguing to themselves, Jesus addressed them, saying, "Why argue in your hearts? Which is the easier thing, to say, 'Your sins are forgiven,' or to say, 'Rise and walk'? But to let you see the Son of man has power on earth to forgive sins"—he said to the paralysed man, "Rise, I tell you, lift your mattress and go home." Instantly he got up before them, lifted what he had been lying on, and went home glorifying God.

NEB—One day he was teaching, and Pharisees and teachers of the law were sitting round. People had come from every village of Galilee and from Judaea and Jerusalem, and the power of the Lord was with him to heal the sick.

Some men appeared carrying a paralysed man on a bed. They tried to bring him in and set him down in front of Jesus, but finding no way to do so because of the crowd, they went up on to the roof and let him down through the tiling, bed and all, into the middle of the company in front of Jesus.

When Jesus saw their faith, he said, 'Man, your sins are forgiven you.' The lawyers and the Pharisees began saying to themselves, 'Who is this fellow with his blasphemous talk? Who but God alone can forgive sins?' But Jesus knew what they were thinking and answered them: 'Why do you harbour thoughts like these? Is it easier to say, "Your sins are forgiven you", or to say, "Stand up and walk"? But to convince you that the Son of Man has the right on earth to forgive sins'—he turned to the paralysed man—'I say to you, stand up, take your bed, and go home.' And at once he rose to his feet before their eyes, took up the bed he had been lying on, and went home praising God.

Healing in the Ministry of Jesus

Luke 6:17-19

KJV—And (Jesus) came down with them, and stood in the plain, and the company of his disciples, and a great multitude of people out of all Judea and Jerusalem, and from the sea coast of Tyre and Sidon, which came to hear him, and to be healed of their diseases; And they that were vexed with unclean spirits: and they were healed. And the whole multitude sought to touch him: for there went virtue out of him, and healed them all.

Amp—And Jesus came down with them and took His stand on a level spot, with a great crowd of His disciples and a vast throng of people from all over Judea and Jerusalem and the seacoast of Tyre and Sidon, who came to listen to Him and to be cured of their diseases; Even those who were disturbed and troubled with unclean spirits, and they were being healed [also]. And all the multitude were seeking to touch Him, for healing power was all the while going forth from Him and cured them all [that is, saving them from severe illnesses or calamities].

Moffatt—With them he came down the hill and stood on a level spot. There was a great company of his disciples with him, and a large multitude of people from all Judaea, from Jerusalem, and from the coast of Tyre and Sidon, who had come to hear him and to get cured of their diseases. Those who were annoyed with unclean spirits also were healed. Indeed the whole of the crowd made efforts to touch him, for power issued from him and cured everybody.

NEB—He came down the hill with them and took his stand on level ground. There was a large concourse of his disciples and great numbers of people from Jerusalem and Judaea and from the seaboard of Tyre and Sidon, who had come to listen to him, and to be cured of their diseases. Those who were troubled with unclean spirits were cured; and everyone in the crowd was trying to touch him, because power went out from him and cured them all.

Luke 7:11-16

KJV—And it came to pass the day after, that (Jesus) went into a city called Nain; and many of his disciples went with him, and much people. Now when he came nigh to the gate of the city, behold, there was a dead man carried out, the only son of his mother, and she was a widow: and much people of the city was with her.

And when the Lord saw her, he had compassion on her, and said unto her, Weep not. And he came and touched the bier: and they that bare him stood still. And he said, Young man, I say unto thee, Arise. And he that was dead sat up, and began to speak. And he delivered him to his mother. And there came a fear on all: and they glorified God, saying, That a great prophet is risen up among us; and, That God hath visited his people.

Amp—Soon afterward Jesus went to a town called Nain, and

His disciples and a great throng accompanied Him. [Just] as He drew near the gate of the town, behold, a man who had died was being carried out, the only son of his mother, and she was a widow; and a large gathering from the town was accompanying her.

And when the Lord saw her, He had compassion on her and said to her, Do not weep. And He went forward and touched the funeral couch, and the pallbearers stood still. And He said, Young man, I say to you, arise [from death]! And the man [who was] dead sat up, and began to speak. And [Jesus] gave him [back] to his mother. Profound and reverent fear seized them all; and they began to recognize God and praise and give thanks, saying, A great prophet has appeared among us! And God has visited His people (in order to help and care for and provide for them)!

Moffatt—It was shortly afterwards that he made his way to a town called Nain, accompanied by his disciples and a large crowd. Just as he was near the gate of the town, there was a dead man being carried out; he was the only son of his mother, and she was a widow. Numbers from the town were with her.

And when the Lord saw her, he felt pity for her and said to her, "Do not weep." Then he went forward and touched the bier; the bearers stopped. "Young man," he said, "I bid you rise." Then the corpse sat up and began to speak; and Jesus gave him back to his mother. All were seized with awe and glorified God. "A great prophet has appeared among us," they said; "God has visited his people."

NEB—Afterwards Jesus went to a town called Nain, accompanied by his disciples and a large crowd. As he approached the gate of the town he met a funeral. The dead man was the only son of his widowed mother; and many of the townspeople were there with her.

When the Lord saw her his heart went out to her, and he said, 'Weep no more.' With that he stepped forward and laid his hand on the bier; and the bearers halted. Then he spoke: 'Young man, rise up!' The dead man sat up and began to speak; and Jesus gave him back to his mother. Deep awe fell upon them all, and they praised God. 'A great prophet has risen among us', they said, and again, 'God has shown his care for his people.'

Luke 13:10-17

KJV—And (Jesus) was teaching in one of the synagogues on the sabbath. And, behold, there was a woman which had a spirit of infirmity eighteen years, and was bowed together, and could in no wise lift up herself. And when Jesus saw her, he called her to him, and said unto her, Woman, thou art loosed from thine infirmity. And he laid his hands on her: and immediately she was made straight, and glorified God.

And the ruler of the synagogue answered with indignation, because that Jesus had healed on the sabbath day, and said unto the people, There are six days in which men ought to work: in them therefore come and be healed, and not on the sabbath day.

The Lord then answered him, and said, Thou hypocrite, doth not each one of you on the sabbath loose his ox or his ass from the stall, and lead him away to watering? And ought not this woman, being a daughter of Abraham, whom Satan hath bound, lo, these eighteen years, be loosed from this bond on the sabbath day? And when he had said these things, all his adversaries were ashamed: and all the people rejoiced for all the glorious things that were done by him.

Amp—Now Jesus was teaching in one of the synagogues on the Sabbath. And there was a woman there who for eighteen years had had an infirmity caused by a spirit [a demon of sickness]. She was bent completely forward and utterly unable to straighten herself or to look upward. And when Jesus saw her, He called [her to Him] and said to her, Woman, you are released from your infirmity! Then He laid [His] hands on her and instantly she was made straight, and she recognized and thanked and praised God.

But the leader of the synagogue, indignant because Jesus had healed on the Sabbath, said to the crowd, There are six days on which work ought to be done, so come on those days and be cured, and not on the Sabbath day.

But the Lord replied to him, saying, You play actors— hypocrites! Does not each one of you on the Sabbath loose his ox or his donkey from the stall, and lead it out to water it? And ought not this woman, a daughter of Abraham whom Satan has kept bound for eighteen years, be loosed from this bond on the Sabbath day? Even as He said this, all His opponents were put to shame, and all the people were rejoicing over all the glorious things that were being done by Him.

Moffatt—When he was teaching in one of the synagogues on the sabbath, there was a woman who for eighteen years had suffered weakness from an evil spirit; indeed she was bent double and could not raise herself at all. Jesus noticed her and called to her, "Woman, you are released from your weakness." He laid his hands on her, and instantly she became erect and glorified God.

But the president of the synagogue was annoyed at Jesus healing on the sabbath, and he said to the crowd, "There are six days for work to be done; come during them to get healed, instead of on the sabbath."

The Lord replied to him, "You hypocrite, does not each of you untether his ox or ass from the stall on the sabbath and lead it away to drink? And this woman, a daughter of Abraham, bound by Satan for all these eighteen years, was she not to be freed from her bondage on the sabbath?" As he said this, all his opponents were put to shame; but as all the crowd rejoiced over all his splendid doings.

NEB—One Sabbath he was teaching in a synagogue, and there was a woman there possessed by a spirit that had crippled her for eighteen years. She was bent double and quite unable to stand up straight. When Jesus saw her he called her and said, 'You are rid of your trouble.' Then he laid his hands on her, and at once she straightened up and began to praise God.

But the president of the synagogue, indignant with Jesus for healing on the Sabbath, intervened and said to the congregation, 'There are six working-days; come and be cured on one of them, and not on the Sabbath.'

The Lord gave him his answer: 'What hypocrites you are!' he said. 'Is there a single one of you who does not loose his ox or his donkey from the manger and take it out to water on the Sabbath? And here is this woman, a daughter of Abraham, who has been kept prisoner by Satan for eighteen long years: was it wrong for her to be freed from her bonds on the Sabbath?' At these words all his opponents were covered with confusion, while the mass of the people were delighted at all the wonderful things he was doing.

Luke 17:11-19

KJV—And it came to pass, as (Jesus) went to Jerusalem, that he passed through the midst of Samaria and Galilee. And as he entered into a certain village, there met him ten men that were lepers, which stood afar off: And they lifted up their voices, and said, Jesus, Master, have mercy on us. And when he saw them, he said unto them, Go show yourselves unto the priests. And it came to pass, that, as they went, they were cleansed.

And one of them, when he saw that he was healed, turned back, and with a loud voice glorified God, And fell down on his face at his feet, giving him thanks: and he was a Samaritan. And

Jesus answering said, Were there not ten cleansed? but where are the nine? There are not found that returned to give glory to God, save this stranger. And he said unto him, Arise, go thy way: thy faith hath made thee whole.

Amp—As He went His way to Jerusalem, it occurred that [Jesus] was passing [along the border] between Samaria and Galilee. And as He was going into one village, He was met by ten lepers, who stood at a distance. And they raised up their voices and called, Jesus, Master, take pity and have mercy on us! And when He saw them He said to them, Go (at once) and show yourselves to the priests. And as they went they were cured and made clean.

Then one of them, upon seeing that he was cured, turned back, recognizing and thanking and praising God with a loud voice; And he fell prostrate at Jesus' feet, thanking Him (over and over). And he was a Samaritan. Then Jesus asked, Were not ten cleansed? Where are the nine? Was there no one found to return and to recognize and give thanks and praise to God except this alien? And He said to him, Get up and go on your way. Your faith [that is, your trust and confidence that spring from your belief in God] has restored you to health.

Moffatt—Now it happened, in the course of his journey to Jerusalem, that he passed between Samaria and Galilee. On entering one village, he was met by ten lepers, who stood at a distance and lifted up their voices, saying, "Jesus, master, have pity on us." Noticing them he said, "Go and show yourselves to the priests." And as they went, they were cleansed.

Now one of them turned back when he saw he had been cured, glorifying God with a loud voice; he fell on his face at the feet of Jesus and thanked him. The man was a Samaritan. So Jesus said, "Were all the ten not cleansed? Where are the other nine? Was there no one to return and give glory to God except this foreigner?" And he said to him, "Get up and go, your faith has made you well."

NEB—In the course of his journey to Jerusalem he was travelling through the borderlands of Samaria and Galilee. As he was entering a village he was met by ten men with leprosy. They stood some way off and called out to him, 'Jesus, Master, take pity on us.' When he saw them he said, 'Go and show yourselves to the priests'; and while they were on their way, they were made clean.

One of them, finding himself cured, turned back praising God aloud. He threw himself down at Jesus's feet and thanked him. And he was a Samaritan. At this Jesus said: 'Were not all ten cleansed? The other nine, where are they? Could none be found to come back and give praise to God except this foreigner?' And he said to the man, 'Stand up and go on your way; your faith has cured you.'

John 5:1-9

KJV—After this there was a feast of the Jews; and Jesus went up to Jerusalem. Now there is at Jerusalem by the sheep market a pool, which is called in the Hebrew tongue Bethesda, having five porches. In these lay a great multitude of impotent folk, of blind, halt, withered, waiting for the moving of the water. For an angel went down at a certain season into the pool, and troubled the water: whosoever then first after the troubling of the water stepped in was made whole of whatsoever disease he had.

And a certain man was there, which had an infirmity thirty and eight years. When Jesus saw him lie, and knew that he had been now a long time in that case, he saith unto him, Wilt thou be made whole? The impotent man answered him, Sir, I have no man, when the water is troubled, to put me into the pool: but while I am coming, another steppeth down before me. Jesus saith unto him, Rise, take up thy bed, and walk. And immediately the man was made whole, and took up his bed, and walked: and on the same day was the sabbath.

Amp—Later on there was a Jewish festival (feast), for which Jesus went up to Jerusalem. Now there is in Jerusalem a pool near the Sheep Gate. This pool in the Hebrew is called Bethesda, having five porches (alcoves, colonnades, doorways). In these lay a great number of sick folk, some blind, some crippled and some paralyzed (shriveled up), waiting for the bubbling up of the water.

There was a certain man there who had suffered with a deepseated and lingering disorder for thirty-eight years. When Jesus noticed him lying there helpless, knowing that he had already been a long time in that condition, He said to him, Do you want to become well? [Are you really in earnest about getting well?] The invalid answered, Sir, I have nobody when the water is moving to put me into the pool; but while I am trying to come myself, somebody else steps down ahead of me. Jesus said to him, Get up; pick up your bed (sleeping pad) and walk! Instantly the man became well and recovered his strength and picked up his bed and walked. But that happened on the Sabbath.

Moffatt—After this there was a festival of the Jews, and Jesus went up to Jerusalem. Now in Jerusalem there is a bath beside the sheep-pool, which is called in Hebrew Bethzatha; it has five porticoes, where a crowd of invalids used to lie, the blind, the lame, and folk with shrivelled limbs [waiting for the water to bubble. For an angel used to descend from time to time into the bath, and disturb the water; whereupon the first person who stepped in after the water was disturbed was restored to health, no matter what disease he had been afflicted with].

Now one man was there, who had been ill for thirty-eight years. Jesus saw him lying, and knowing he had been ill for a long while he said to him, "Do you want your health restored?"

The invalid replied, "Sir, I have nobody to put me into the bath, when the water is disturbed; and while I am getting down myself, someone else gets in before me." Jesus said to him, "Get up, lift your mat, and walk." And instantly the man got well, lifted his mat, and started to walk. Now it was the sabbath on that day.

NEB—Later on Jesus went up to Jerusalem for one of the Jewish festivals. Now at the Sheep-Pool in Jerusalem there is a place with five colonnades. Its name in the language of the Jews is Bethesda. In these colonnades there lay a crowd of sick people, blind, lame, and paralysed.

Among them was a man who had been crippled for thirty-eight years. When Jesus saw him lying there and was aware that he had been ill a long time, he asked him, 'Do you want to recover?' 'Sir,' he replied, 'I have no one to put me in the pool when the water is disturbed, but while I am moving, someone else is in the pool before me.' Jesus answered, 'Rise to your feet, take up your bed and walk.' The man recovered instantly, took up his stretcher, and began to walk. That day was a Sabbath.

Acts 10:38

KJV—How God anointed Jesus of Nazareth with the Holy Ghost and with power: who went about doing good, and healing all that were oppressed of the devil; for God was with him.

Amp—How God anointed and consecrated Jesus of Nazareth with the (Holy) Spirit and with strength and ability and power; how He went about doing good and in particular curing all that were harassed and oppressed by [the power of] the devil, for God was with Him.

Moffatt—How God consecrated Jesus of Nazareth with the holy Spirit and power, and how he went about doing good and curing all who were harassed by the devil; for God was with him.

NEB—You know about Jesus of Nazareth, how God anointed him with the Holy Spirit and with power. He went about doing good and healing all who were oppressed by the devil, for God was with him.

***

Healing by the
Disciples and Apostles

Healing is an
inseparable part of the
gospel. So when Jesus
sent His disciples to
preach the good news, He
also commissioned them
to heal the sick.

John 14:12

KJV—Verily, verily, I say unto you, He that believeth on me, the works that I do shall he do also; and greater works than these shall he do; because I go unto my Father.

Amp—I assure you, most solemnly I tell you, if any one steadfastly believes in Me, he will himself be able to do the things that I do; and he will do even greater things than these, because I go to the Father.

Moffatt—Truly, truly I tell you, he who believes in me will do the very deeds I do, and still greater deeds than these. For I am going to the Father.

NEB—In truth, in very truth I tell you, he who has faith in me will do what I am doing; and he will do greater things still because I am going to the Father.

Mark 6:7, 12-13

KJV—And (Jesus) called unto him the twelve, and began to send them forth by two and two; and gave them power over unclean spirits...And they went out, and preached that men should repent. And they cast out many devils, and anointed with oil many that were sick, and healed them.

Amp—And He called to Him the twelve [apostles]; and began to send them out [as His ambassadors] two by two, and gave them authority and power over the unclean spirits...So they went out and preached that men should repent [that is that they should change their minds for the better, and heartily amend their ways with abhorrence for their past sins]. And they drove out many unclean spirits, and anointed with oil many who were sick, and cured them.

Moffatt—And summoning the twelve he proceeded to send

them out two by two; he gave them power over the unclean spirits...So they went out and preached repentance; also they cast out a number of daemons, and cured a number of sick people by anointing them with oil.

NEB—On one of his teaching journeys round the villages he summoned the Twelve and sent them out in pairs on a mission. He gave them authority over unclean spirits...So they sent out and called publicly for repentance. They drove out many devils, and many sick people they anointed with oil and cured.

Mark 16:14-18

KJV—(After Jesus' resurrection) he appeared unto the eleven as they sat at meat, and upbraided them with their unbelief and hardness of heart, because they believed not them which had seen him after he was risen.

And he said unto them, Go ye into all the world, and preach the gospel to every creature. He that believeth and is baptized shall be saved; but he that believeth not shall be damned. And these signs shall follow them that believe; In my name shall they cast out devils; they shall speak with new tongues; They shall take up serpents; and if they drink any deadly thing, it shall not hurt them; they shall lay hands on the sick, and they shall recover.

Amp—Afterward He appeared to the eleven [apostles, themselves] as they reclined at table; and He reproved and reproached them for their unbelief (their lack of faith) and their hardness of heart, because they had refused to believe those who had seen Him and looked at Him attentively after He was risen (from death).

And He said to them, Go into all the world and preach and publish openly the good news (the Gospel) to every creature (of the whole human race). He who believes—[that is,] who adheres to and trusts in and relies on the Gospel and Him Whom it sets forth—and is baptized will be saved [from the penalty of eternal death]; but he who does not believe—who does not adhere to and trust in and rely on the Gospel and Him Whom it sets forth—will be condemned. And these attesting signs will accompany those who believe: in My name they will drive out demons; they will speak in new languages; They will pick up serpents, and [even] if they drink anything deadly, it will not hurt them; they will lay their hands on the sick, and they will get well.

Moffatt—Afterwards he appeared at table to the eleven themselves and reproached them for their unbelief and dulness of mind, because they had not believed those who saw him risen from the dead. [But they excused themselves, saying, "This age of lawlessness and unbelief lies under the sway of Satan, who will not allow what lies under the unclean spirits to understand the truth and power of God; therefore," they said to Christ, "reveal your righteousness now." Christ answered them, "The term of years for Satan's power has now expired, but other terrors are at hand. I was delivered to death on behalf of sinners, that they might return to the truth and sin no more, that they might inherit that glory of righteousness which is spiritual and imperishable in heaven."]

And he said to them, "Go to all the world and preach the gospel to every creature: he who believes and is baptized shall be saved, but he who will not believe shall be condemned. And for those who believe, these miracles will follow: they will cast out daemons in my name, they will talk in foreign tongues, they will handle serpents, and if they drink any deadly poison, it will not hurt them; they will lay hands on the sick and make them well."

NEB—Afterwards while the Eleven were at table he appeared to them and reproached them for their incredulity and dullness, because they had not believed those who had seen him after he was raised from the dead.

Then he said to them: 'Go forth to every part of the world, and proclaim the Good News to the whole creation. Those who believe it and receive baptism will find salvation; those who do not believe will be condemned. Faith will bring with it these miracles: believers will cast out devils in my name and speak in strange tongues; if they handle snakes or drink any deadly poison, they will come to no harm; and the sick on whom they lay their hands will recover.'

Luke 9:1-2, 6

KJV—Then (Jesus) called his twelve disciples together, and gave them power and authority over all devils, and to cure diseases. And he sent them to preach the kingdom of God, and to heal the sick...And they departed, and went through the towns, preaching the gospel, and healing every where.

Amp—Then Jesus called together the twelve apostles, and gave them power and authority over all demons and to cure diseases, And He sent them out to announce and preach the kingdom of God and to bring healing...And departing they went about from village to village, preaching the Gospel and restoring the afflicted to health everywhere.

Moffatt—Calling the twelve apostles together, he gave them power and authority over all daemons as well as to heal diseases, sending them out to preach the Reign of God and to cure the sick...So they went from village to village, preaching the gospel and healing everywhere.

NEB—He now called the Twelve together and gave them power and authority to overcome all the devils and to cure diseases, and sent them to proclaim the kingdom of God and to heal...So they set out and travelled from village to village, and everywhere they told the good news and healed the sick.

Luke 10:1-3, 8-9

KJV—After these things the Lord appointed other seventy also, and sent them two and two before his face into every city and place, whither he himself would come. Therefore said he unto them, The harvest truly is great, but the labourers are few: pray ye therefore the Lord of the harvest, that he would send forth laborers into his harvest. Go your ways... And into whatsoever city ye enter, and they receive you, eat such things as are set before you: And heal the sick that are therein, and say unto them, The kingdom of God is come nigh unto you.

Amp—Now after this the Lord chose and appointed seventy others, and sent them out ahead of Him, two by two, into every town and place where He Himself was about to come (visit). And He said to them, (There is much ripe grain,) the harvest indeed is abundant, but the farm hands are few. Pray therefore the Lord of the harvest to send out laborers into His harvest. Go your way; behold...Whenever you go into a town and they receive and accept and welcome you, eat what is set before you; And heal the sick in it and say to them, The kingdom of God has come close to you.

Moffatt—After that the Lord commissioned other seventy disciples, sending them in front of him two by two to every town and place that he intended to visit himself. He said to them, "The harvest is rich, but the labourers are few; so pray the Lord of the harvest to send labourers to gather his harvest. Go your way...Wherever you are received, on entering any town, eat what is provided for you, heal those in the town who are ill, and tell them, 'The Reign of God is nearly on you.'"

NEB—After this the Lord appointed a further seventy-two and sent them on ahead in pairs to every town and place he was going to visit himself. He said to them: 'The crop is heavy, but labourers are scarce: you must therefore beg the owner to send labourers to harvest his crop. Be on your way.'...Do not move from house to house. When you come into a town and they make you welcome, eat the food provided for you; heal the sick there, and say, "The kingdom of God has come close to you."

Acts 3:1-10

KJV—Now Peter and John went up together into the temple at the hour of prayer, being the ninth hour. And a certain man lame from his mother's womb was carried, whom they laid daily at the gate of the temple which is called Beautiful, to ask alms of them that entered into the temple; Who seeing Peter and John about to go into the temple asked an alms.

And Peter, fastening his eyes upon him with John, said, Look on us. And he gave heed unto them, expecting to receive something of them. Then Peter said, Silver and gold have I none; but such as I have give I thee: In the name of Jesus Christ of Nazareth rise up and walk.

And he took him by the right hand, and lifted him up: and immediately his feet and ankle bones received strength. And he leaping up stood, and walked, and entered with them into the temple, walking, and leaping, and praising God. And all the people saw him walking and praising God: And they knew that it was he which sat for alms at the Beautiful gate of the temple: and they were filled with wonder and amazement at that which had happened unto him.

Amp—Now Peter and John were going up to the temple at the hour of prayer, the ninth hour (three o'clock in the afternoon), [When] a certain man crippled from his birth was being carried along, who was laid each day at that gate of the temple [which is] called Beautiful, that he might beg for charitable gifts from those who entered the temple. So when he saw Peter and John about to go into the temple, he asked them to give him a gift.

And Peter directed his gaze intently at him, and so did John, and said, Look at us! And [the man] paid attention to them, expecting that he was going to get something from them. But Peter said, Silver and gold [money], I have none; but what I do have, that I give to you: in (the use of) the name of Jesus Christ of Nazareth, walk!

Then he took hold of the man's right hand with a firm grip and raised him up. And at once his feet and ankle bones became strong and steady, And leaping forth he stood and began to walk, and he went into the temple with them, walking and leap-ing and praising God. And all the people saw him walking about and praising God, And they recognized him as the man who usu-ally sat [begging] for alms at the Beautiful Gate of the temple, and they were filled with wonder and amazement (bewilder-ment, consternation) over what had occurred to him.

Moffatt—Peter and John were on their way up to the temple for the hour of prayer at three in the afternoon, when a man lame from birth was carried past, who used to be laid every day at what was called the 'Beautiful Gate' of the temple, to ask alms from those who entered the temple. When he noticed that Peter and John meant to go into the temple, he asked them for alms.

Peter looked at him steadily, as did John, and said, "Look at us." The man attended, expecting to get something from them. But Peter said, "I have no silver or gold, but I will give you what I do have. In the name of Jesus Christ the Nazarene, get up and walk!"

And catching him by the right hand he raised him. Instantly his feet and ankles grew strong, he leapt to his feet, started to walk, and accompanied them into the temple, walking, leaping, and praising God. When all the people saw him walking and praising God, and when they recognized that this was the very man who used to sit and beg at the Gate Beautiful, they were lost in awe and amazement at what had happened to him.

NEB—One day at three in the afternoon, the hour of prayer, Peter and John were on their way up to the temple. Now a man who had been a cripple from birth used to be carried there and laid everyday by the gate of the temple called 'Beautiful Gate', to beg from people as they went in. When he saw Peter and John on their way into the temple he asked for charity.

But Peter fixed his eyes on him, as John did also, and said, 'Look at us.' Expecting a gift from them, the man was all attention. And Peter said, 'I have no silver or gold; but what I have I give you: in the name of Jesus Christ of Nazareth, walk.'

Then he grasped him by the right hand and pulled him up; and at once his feet and ankles grew strong; he sprang up, stood on his feet, and started to walk. He entered the temple with them, leaping and praising God as he went. Everyone saw him walking and praising God, and when they recognized him as the man who used to sit begging at Beautiful Gate, they were filled with wonder and amazement at what had happened to him.

Acts 5:12-16

KJV—And by the hands of the apostles were many signs and wonders wrought among the people; (and they were all with one accord in Solomon's porch. And of the rest durst no man join himself to them: but the people magnified them. And believers were the more added to the Lord, multitudes both of men and women.)

Insomuch that they brought forth the sick into the streets,

and laid them on beds and couches, that at the least the shadow of Peter passing by might overshadow some of them. There came also a multitude out of the cities round about unto Jerusalem, bringing sick folks, and them which were vexed with unclean spirits: and they were healed every one.

Amp—Now by the hands of the apostles (special messengers) numerous and startling signs and wonders were being performed among the people. And by common consent they all met together [at the temple] in the porch or covered walk called Solomon's. And none of those who were not of their number dared to join and associate with them, but the people held them in high regard and praised and made much of them. More and more there were being added to the Lord those who believed—[that is,] those who acknowledged Jesus as their Savior and devoted themselves to Him, joined and gathered with them—crowds both of men and of women.

So that they [even] kept carrying out the sick into the streets and placing them on couches and sleeping pads, [in the hope] that as Peter passed by at least his shadow might fall on some of them. And the people gathered also from the towns and hamlets around Jerusalem, bringing the sick and those troubled with foul spirits, and they were all cured.

Moffatt—Now they all without exception met in the portico of Solomon. Though the people extolled them, not a soul from the outside dared to join them. On the other hand, crowds of men and women who believed in the Lord were brought in. Many miracles and wonders were performed among the people by the apostles. In fact, invalids were actually carried into the streets and laid on beds and mattresses, so that, when Peter passed, his shadow at anyrate might fall on one or other of them. Crowds gathered even from the towns near Jerusalem, bringing invalids and people troubled with unclean spirits, all of whom were healed.

NEB—And many remarkable and wonderful things took place among the people at the hands of the apostles. They used to meet by common consent in Solomon's Portico, no one from outside their number venturing to join with them. But people in general spoke highly of them, and more than that, numbers of men and women were added to their ranks as believers in the Lord.

In the end the sick were actually carried out into the streets and laid there on beds and stretchers, so that even the shadow of Peter might fall on one or another as he passed by; and the people from the towns round Jerusalem flocked in, bringing those who were ill or harassed by unclean spirits, and all of them were cured.

Acts 8:5-8

KJV—Then Philip went down to the city of Samaria, and preached Christ unto them. And the people with one accord gave heed unto those things which Philip spake, hearing and seeing the miracles which he did. For unclean spirits, crying with loud voice, came out of many that were possessed with them: and many taken with palsies, and that were lame, were healed. And there was great joy in that city.

Amp—Philip [the deacon, not the apostle] went down to the city of Samaria, and proclaimed the Christ, the Messiah, to them [the people]; And great crowds of people with one accord listened to and heeded what was said by Philip, as they heard him and watched the miracles and wonders which he kept performing [from time to time]. For foul spirits came out of many who were possessed by them, screaming and shouting with a loud voice, and many who were suffering from palsy or were crippled were restored to health. And there was great rejoicing in that city.

Moffatt—Philip travelled down to a town in Samaria, where he preached Christ to the people. And the crowds attended like one man to what was said by Philip, listening to him and watching the miracles he performed. For unclean spirits came screaming and shrieking out of many who had been possessed, and many paralytics and lame people were healed. So there was great rejoicing in that town.

NEB—Philip came down to a city in Samaria and began proclaiming the Messiah to them. The crowds, to a man, listened eagerly to what Philip said, when they heard him and saw the miracles that he performed. For in many cases of possession the unclean spirits came out with a loud cry; and many paralysed and crippled folk were cured; and there was great joy in that city.

Acts 9:32-34

KJV—And it came to pass, as Peter passed throughout all quarters, he came down also to the saints which dwelt at Lydda. And there he found a certain man named Aeneas, which had kept his bed eight years, and was sick of the palsy. And Peter said unto him, Aeneas, Jesus Christ maketh thee whole: arise, and make thy bed. And he arose immediately.

Amp—Now as Peter went here and there among them all, he went down also to the saints who lived at Lydda. There he found a man named Aeneas, who had been bedfast for eight years and was paralyzed. And Peter said to him, Aeneas, Jesus Christ, the Messiah, [now] makes you whole. Get up and make your bed! And immediately [Aeneas] stood up.

Moffatt—Peter moved here and there among them all, and it happened that in the course of his tours he came down to visit the saints who stayed at Lydda. There he found a man called Aeneas who had been bed-ridden for eight years with paralysis. "Aeneas," said Peter, "Jesus the Christ cures you! Get up and make your bed!" He got up at once.

NEB—Peter was making a general tour, in the course of which he went down to visit God's people at Lydda. There he found a man named Aeneas who had been bedridden with paralysis for eight years. Peter said to him, 'Aeneas, Jesus Christ cures you; get up and make your bed', and immediately he stood up.

Acts 14:8-10

KJV—And there sat a certain man at Lystra, impotent in his feet, being a cripple from his mother's womb, who never had walked: The same heard Paul speak: who steadfastly beholding him, and perceiving that he had faith to be healed, Said with a loud voice, Stand upright on thy feet. And he leaped and walked.

Amp—Now at Lystra a man sat whose feet it was impossible for him to use, for he was a cripple from birth and had never walked. He was listening to Paul as he talked, and [Paul] gazing intently at him and observing that he had faith to be healed, Shouted at him, saying, Stand erect on your feet! And he leaped up and walked.

Moffatt—At Lystra there was a man sitting, who was powerless in his feet, a lame man unable to walk ever since he was born. He heard Paul speaking, and Paul, gazing steadily at him and noticing that he had faith enough to make him better, said in a loud voice, "Stand erect on your feet." Up he jumped and began to walk.

NEB—At Lystra sat a crippled man, lame from birth, who

had never walked in his life. This man listened while Paul was speaking. Paul fixed his eyes on him and saw that he had the faith to be cured, so he said to him in a loud voice, 'Stand up straight on your feet'; and he sprang up and started to walk.

Acts 19:11-12

KJV—And God wrought special miracles by the hands of Paul: So that from his body were brought unto the sick handkerchiefs or aprons, and the diseases departed from them, and the evil spirits went out of them.

Amp—And God did unusual and extraordinary miracles by the hands of Paul, So that handkerchiefs or towels or aprons which had touched his skin were carried away and put upon the sick, and their diseases left them, and the evil spirits came out of them.

Moffatt—God also worked no ordinary miracles by means of Paul; people even carried away towels or aprons he had used, and at their touch sick folk were freed from their diseases and evil spirits came out of them.

NEB—And through Paul God worked singular miracles: when handkerchiefs and scarves which had been in contact with his skin were carried to the sick, they were rid of their diseases and the evil spirits came out of them.

Acts 28:8-9

KJV—And it came to pass, that the father of Publius lay sick of a fever and of a bloody flux: to whom Paul entered in, and prayed, and laid his hands on him, and healed him. So when this was done, others also, which had diseases in the island, came, and were healed.

Amp—And it happened that the father of Publius was sick

in bed with recurring attacks of fever and dysentery; and Paul went to see him, and after praying and laying his hands on him he healed him. After this had occurred, the other people on the island who had diseases also kept coming and were cured.

Moffatt—His father, it so happened, was laid up with fever and dysentery, but Paul went in to see him and after prayer laid his hands on him and cured him. When this had happened, the rest of the sick folk in the island also came and got cured.

NEB—It so happened that this man's father was in bed suffering from recurrent bouts of fever and dysentery. Paul visited him and, after prayer, laid his hands upon him and healed him; whereupon the other sick people on the island came also and were cured.

***

Healing in the
Church Today

Healing is your right
as a born-again child
of God. Throughout
the New Testament,
God reminds us of that
inheritance and exhorts
us to live in the
fullness of it.

1 Thessalonians 5:23-24

KJV—And the very God of peace sanctify you wholly; and I pray God your whole spirit and soul and body be preserved blameless unto the coming of our Lord Jesus Christ. Faithful is he that calleth you, who also will do it.

Amp—And may the God of peace Himself sanctify you through and through—that is, separate you from profane things, make you pure and wholly consecrated to God—and may your spirit and soul and body be preserved sound and complete [and found] blameless at the coming of our Lord Jesus Christ, the Messiah. Faithful is He Who is calling you [to Himself] and utterly trustworthy, and He will also do it [that is, fulfill His call by hallowing and keeping you].

Moffatt—May the God of peace consecrate you through and through! Spirit, soul, and body, may you be kept without break or blame till the arrival of our Lord Jesus Christ! He who calls you is faithful, he will do this.

NEB—May God himself, the God of peace, make you holy in every part, and keep you sound in spirit, soul, and body, without fault when our Lord Jesus Christ comes. He who calls you is to be trusted; he will do it.

2 Timothy 1:7

KJV—For God hath not given us the spirit of fear; but of power, and of love, and of a sound mind.

Amp—For God did not give us a spirit of timidity—of cowardice, of craven and cringing and fawning fear—but [He has given us a spirit] of power and of love and of calm and well-balanced mind and discipline and self-control.

Moffatt—For God has not given us a timid spirit but a spirit of power and love and discipline.

NEB—For the spirit that God gave us is no craven spirit, but one to inspire strength, love, and self-discipline.

James 5:14-16

KJV—Is any sick among you? let him call for the elders of the church; and let them pray over him, anointing him with oil in the name of the Lord: And the prayer of faith shall save the sick, and the Lord shall raise him up; and if he have committed sins, they shall be forgiven him. Confess your faults one to another, and pray one for another, that ye may be healed. The effectual fervent prayer of a righteous man availeth much.

Amp—Is any one among you sick? He should call in the church elders—the spiritual guides. And they should pray over him, anointing him with oil in the Lord's name. And the prayer [that is] of faith will save him that is sick, and the Lord will restore him; and if he has committed sins, he will be forgiven. Confess to one another therefore your faults—your slips, your false steps, your offenses, your sins; and pray [also] for one another, that you may be healed and restored—to a spiritual tone of mind and heart. The earnest (heartfelt, continued) prayer of a righteous man makes tremendous power available—dynamic in its working.

Moffatt—Is anyone ill? let him summon the presbyters of the church, and let them pray over him, anointing him with oil in the name of the Lord; the prayer of faith will restore the sick man, and the Lord will raise him up; even the sins he has committed will be forgiven him. So confess your sins to one another and pray for one another, that you may be healed; the prayers of the righteous have a powerful effect.

NEB—Is one of you ill? He should send for the elders of the congregation to pray over him and anoint him with oil in the name of the Lord. The prayer offered in faith will save the sick man, the Lord will raise him from his bed, and any sins he may have committed will be forgiven. Therefore confess your sins to one another, and pray for one another, and then you will be healed. A good man's prayer is powerful and effective.

2 Peter 1:2-4

KJV—Grace and peace be multiplied unto you through the knowledge of God, and of Jesus our Lord, According as his divine power hath given unto us all things that pertain unto life and godliness, through the knowledge of him that hath called us to glory and virtue: Whereby are given unto us exceeding great and precious promises: that by these ye might be partakers of the divine nature, having escaped the corruption that is in the world through lust.

Amp—May grace (God's favor) and peace, (which is perfect well-being, all necessary good, all spiritual prosperity and freedom from fears and agitating passions and moral conflicts) be multiplied to you in (the full, personal, precise and correct) knowledge of God and of Jesus our Lord. For His divine power has bestowed upon us all things that [are requisite and suited] to life and godliness, through the (full, personal) knowledge of Him Who called us by and to His own glory and excellence (virtue).

By means of these He has bestowed on us His precious and exceedingly great promises, so that through them you may escape (by flight) from the moral decay (rottenness and corruption) that is in the world because of covetousness (lust and greed), and become sharers (partakers) of the divine nature.

Moffatt—Grace and peace be multiplied to you by the knowledge of our Lord. Inasmuch as his power divine has bestowed upon us every requisite for life and godliness by the knowledge of him who called us to his own glory and excellence—bestowing on us thereby promises precious and supreme, that by means of them you may escape the corruption produced within the world by lust, and participate in the divine nature.

NEB—Grace and peace be yours in fullest measure, through the knowledge of God and Jesus our Lord. His divine power has bestowed on us everything that makes for life and true religion, enabling us to know the One who called us by his own splendour and might. Through this might and splendour he has given us his promises, great beyond all price, and through them you may escape the corruption with which lust has infected the world, and come to share in the very being of God.

3 John 2

KJV—Beloved, I wish above all things that thou mayest prosper and be in health, even as thy soul prospereth.

Amp—Beloved, I pray that you may prosper in every way and [that your body] may keep well, even as [I know] your soul keeps well and prospers.

Moffatt—Beloved, I pray you may prosper in every way and keep well—as indeed your soul is keeping well.

NEB—My dear Gaius, I pray that you may enjoy good health, and that all may go well with you, as I know it goes well with your soul.

***

Receive Healing by
Faith in the Word

*Even though healing
is God's unchangeable
will for you, it does not
come automatically. You
must receive it, just as
you received your new
birth—by faith
in God's Word*

Galatians 3:5

KJV—He therefore that ministereth to you the Spirit, and worketh miracles among you, doeth he it by the works of the law, or by the hearing of faith?

Amp—Then does He Who supplies you with His marvelous (Holy) Spirit, and works powerfully and miraculously among you, [do so on the grounds of your doing] what the Law demands, or because of your believing and adhering to and trusting in and relying on the message that you heard?

Moffatt—When He supplies you with the Spirit and works miracles among you, is it because you do what the Law commands or because you believe the gospel message?

NEB—I ask then: when God gives you the Spirit and works miracles among you, why is this? Is it because you keep the law, or is it because you have faith in the gospel message?

Proverbs 4:20-24

KJV—My son, attend to my words; incline thine ear unto my sayings. Let them not depart from thine eyes; keep them in the midst of thine heart. For they are life unto those that find them, and health to all their flesh. Keep thy heart with all diligence; for out of it are the issues of life. Put away from thee a froward mouth, and perverse lips put far from thee.

Amp—My son, attend to my words; consent and submit to my sayings. Let them not depart from your sight; keep them in the center of your heart. For they are life to those who find them, healing and health to all their flesh. Keep your heart with all vigilance and above all that you guard, for out of it flow the springs of life. Put away from you false and dishonest speech, and willful and contrary talk put far from you.

Moffatt—My son, attend to what I say, bend your ear to my words; never lose sight of them, but fix them in your mind; to those who find them, they are life, and health to all their being. Guard above all things, guard your inner self, for so you live and prosper; bar out all talk of evil, and banish wayward words.

NEB—My son, attend to my speech, pay heed to my words; do not let them slip out of your mind, keep them close in your heart; for they are life to him who finds them, and health to his whole body. Guard your heart more than any treasure, for it is the source of all life. Keep your mouth from crooked speech and your lips from deceitful talk.

Isaiah 55:7-11

KJV—Let the wicked forsake his way, and the unrighteous man his thoughts: and let him return unto the Lord, and he will have mercy upon him; and to our God, for he will abundantly pardon.

For my thoughts are not your thoughts, neither are your ways my ways, saith the Lord. For as the heavens are higher than the earth, so are my ways higher than your ways, and my thoughts than your thoughts. For as the rain cometh down, and the snow from heaven, and returneth not thither, but watereth the earth, and maketh it bring forth and bud, that it may give seed to the sower, and bread to the eater: So shall my word be that goeth forth out of my mouth: it shall not return unto me void, but it shall accomplish that which I please, and it shall prosper in the thing whereto I sent it.

Amp—Let the wicked forsake his way, and the unrighteous man his thoughts; and let him return to the Lord, and He will have love, pity and mercy for him; and to our God, for He will multiply to him His abundant pardon.

For My thoughts are not your thoughts, neither are your

ways My ways, says the Lord. For as the heavens are higher than the earth, so are My ways higher than your ways, and My thoughts than your thoughts. For as the rain and snow come down from the heavens, and return not there again, but water the earth and make it bring forth and sprout, that it may give seed to the sower and bread to the eater, So shall My word be that goes forth out of My mouth; it shall not return to Me void—without producing any effect, useless—but it shall accomplish that which I please and purpose, and it shall prosper in the thing for which I sent it.

Moffatt—Let guilty men give up their ways, and evil men their purposes; let them turn back to the Eternal, who will pity them, turn back to our God, for he will pardon them abundantly.

For my plans are not like your plans, nor your ways like my ways—so the Eternal One declares; nay, as heaven is higher than the earth, so are my ways higher than your ways, and my plans than your plans. As rain and snow from heaven fall not in vain, but water earth until it yields seed for the sower, food for hungry men, so with the promise that has passed my lips: it falls not fruitless and in vain, but works out what I will, and carries out my purpose.

NEB—Let the wicked abandon their ways and evil men their thoughts: let them return to the Lord, who will have pity on them, return to our God, for he will freely forgive.

For my thoughts are not your thoughts, and your ways are not my ways. This is the very word of the Lord. For as the heavens are higher than the earth, so are my ways higher than your ways and my thoughts than your thoughts; and as the rain and the snow come down from heaven and do not return until they have watered the earth, making it blossom and bear fruit, and give seed for sowing and bread to eat, so shall the word which comes from my mouth prevail; it shall not return to me fruitless without accomplishing my purpose or succeeding in the task I gave it.

Matthew 15:6

KJV—Thus have ye made the commandment of God of none effect by your tradition.

Amp—So for the sake of your tradition (the rules handed down by your forefathers), you have set aside the Word of God—depriving it of force and authority and making it of no effect.

Moffatt—So you have repealed the law of God to suit your own tradition.

NEB—You have made God's law null and void out of respect for your tradition.

Romans 10:17

KJV—So then faith cometh by hearing, and hearing by the word of God.

Amp—So faith comes by hearing [what is told], and what is heard comes by the preaching [of the message that came from the lips] of Christ, the Messiah [Himself].

Moffatt—(You see, faith must come from what is heard, and what is heard comes from word of Christ.)

NEB—We conclude that faith is awakened by the message, and the message that awakens it comes through the word of Christ.

Mark 4:24

KJV—And he said unto them, Take heed what ye hear: with what measure ye mete, it shall be measured to you: and unto you that hear shall more be given.

Amp—And He said to them, Be careful what you are hearing. The measure [of thought and study] you give [to the truth you hear] will be the measure [of virtue and knowledge] that comes back to you, and more [besides] will be given to you who hear.

Moffatt—Also he said to them, "Take care what you hear; the measure you deal out to others will be dealt out to yourselves, and you will receive extra."

NEB—He also said, "Take note of what you hear; the measure you give is the measure you will receive, with something more besides."

Psalm 107:20

KJV—(The Lord) sent his word, and healed them, and delivered them from their destructions.

Amp—He sends forth His word and heals them and rescues them from the pit and destruction.

Moffatt—He sent his word to heal them and preserve their life.

NEB—He sent his word to heal them and bring them alive out of the pit of death.

***

*Once you have planted God's healing Word in
your heart, you can pray with confidence, knowing you will receive your healing. Yet, to get results, you must believe you receive when you pray. That is
when God's healing power is released in your body.*

Mark 11:22-24

KJV—And Jesus answering saith unto them, Have faith in God. For verily I say unto you, That whosoever shall say unto this mountain, Be thou removed, and be thou cast into the sea; and shall not doubt in his heart, but shall believe that those things which he saith shall come to pass; he shall have whatsoever he saith. Therefore I say unto you, What things soever ye desire, when ye pray, believe that ye receive them, and ye shall have them.

Amp—And Jesus replying said to them, Have faith in God (constantly). Truly, I tell you, whoever says to this mountain, Be lifted up and thrown into the sea! and does not doubt at all in his heart, but believes that what he says will take place, it will be done for him. For this reason I am telling you, whatever you ask for in prayer, believe—trust and be confident—that it is granted to you, and you will [get it].

Moffatt—Jesus answered them, "Have faith in God! I tell you truly, whoever says to this hill, 'Take and throw yourself into the sea,' and has not a doubt in his mind but believes that what he says will happen, he will have it done. So I tell you, whatever you pray for and ask, believe you have got it, and you shall have it."

NEB—Jesus answered them, 'Have faith in God. I tell you this: if anyone says to this mountain, "Be lifted from your place and hurled into the sea", and has no inward doubts, but believes that what he says is happening, it will be done for him. I tell you, then, whatever you ask for in prayer, believe that you have received it and it will be yours.'

Mark 6:5-6

KJV—And he could there do no mighty work, save that he laid his hands upon a few sick folk, and healed them. And he marvelled because of their unbelief.

Amp—And He was not able to do even one work of power there, except that He laid His hands on a few sickly people [and] cured them. And He marveled because of their unbelief—their lack of faith in Him.

Moffatt—There he could not do any miracle, beyond laying his hands on a few sick people and curing them. He was astonished at their lack of faith.

NEB—He could work no miracle there, except that he put his hands on a few sick people and healed them; and he was taken aback by their want of faith.

Matthew 18:18-19

KJV—Verily I say unto you, Whatsoever ye shall bind on earth shall be bound in heaven: and whatsoever ye shall loose on earth shall be loosed in heaven. Again I say unto you, That if two of you shall agree on earth as touching any thing that they shall ask, it shall be done for them of my Father which is in heaven.

Amp—Truly, I tell you, whatever you forbid and declare to be improper and unlawful on earth must be what is already forbidden in heaven, and whatever you permit and declare proper and lawful on earth must be already permitted in heaven. Again I tell you, if two of you on earth agree (harmonize together, together make a symphony) about—anything and everything—whatever they shall ask, it will come to pass and be done for them by My Father in heaven.

Moffatt—I tell you truly, Whatever you prohibit on earth will be prohibited in heaven, and whatever you permit on earth will be permitted in heaven. I tell you another thing: if two of you agree on earth about anything you pray for, it will be done for you by my Father in heaven.

NEB—'I tell you this: whatever you forbid on earth shall be forbidden in heaven, and whatever you allow on earth shall be allowed in heaven. 'Again I tell you this: if two of you agree on earth about any request you have to make, that request will be granted by my heavenly Father.'

Matthew 21:21

KJV—Jesus answered and said unto them, Verily I say unto you, If ye have faith, and doubt not, ye shall not only do this which is done to the fig tree, but also if ye shall say unto this mountain, Be thou removed, and be thou cast into the sea; it shall be done.

Amp—And Jesus answered them, Truly, I say to you, if you have faith—a firm relying trust—and do not doubt, you will not only do what has been done to the fig tree, but even if you say to this mountain, Be taken up and cast into the sea, it will be done.

Moffatt—Jesus answered, "I tell you truly, if you have faith, if you have no doubt, you will not only do what has been done to the fig tree, but even if you say to this hill, 'Take and throw yourself into the sea,' it will be done."

NEB—Jesus answered them, 'I tell you this: if only you have faith and have no doubts, you will do what has been done to the fig-tree; and more than that, you need only say to this mountain, "Be lifted from your place and hurled into the sea", and what you say will be done.'

John 15:7

KJV—If ye abide in me, and my words abide in you, ye shall ask what ye will, and it shall be done unto you.

Amp—If you live in Me—abide vitally united to Me—and My words remain in you and continue to live in your hearts, ask whatever you will and it shall be done for you.

Moffatt—If you remain in me and my words remain in you, then ask whatever you like and you shall have it.

NEB—If you dwell in me, and my words dwell in you, ask what you will, and you shall have it.

1 John 5:14-15

KJV—And this is the confidence that we have in him, that, if we ask any thing according to his will, he heareth us: And if we know that he hear us, whatsoever we ask, we know that we have the petitions that we desired of him.

Amp—And this is the confidence—the assurance, the [privilege of] boldness—which we have in Him: [we are sure] that if we ask anything (make any request) according to His will (in agreement with His own plan) He listens to and hears us. And if (since) we [positively] know that He listens to us in whatever we ask, we also know [with settled and absolute knowledge] that we have [granted us as our present possessions] the requests made of Him.

Moffatt—Now the confidence we have in him is this, that he listens to us whenever we ask anything in accordance with his will; and if we know that he listens to whatever we ask, we know that we obtain the requests we have made to him.

NEB—We can approach God with confidence for this reason: if we make requests which accord with his will he listens to us; and if we know that our requests are heard, we know also that the things we ask for are ours.

***

The Communion elements are powerful symbols of
the body and blood of Jesus that ratified our covenant with God in Him.
Taking Communion and reminding yourself of the blood covenant can help
stop unbelief more than anything else.

Hebrews 6:16-20

KJV—For men verily swear by the greater: and an oath for confirmation is to them an end of all strife. Wherein God, willing more abundantly to show unto the heirs of promise the immutability of his counsel, confirmed it by an oath: That by two immutable things, in which it was impossible for God to lie, we might have a strong consolation, who have fled for refuge to lay hold upon the hope set before us: Which hope we have as an anchor of the soul, both sure and steadfast, and which entereth into that within the veil; Whither the forerunner is for us entered, even Jesus, made an high priest for ever after the order of Melchisedec.

Amp—Men indeed swear by a greater [than themselves], and with them in all disputes the oath taken for confirmation is final—ending strife. Accordingly God also, in His desire to show more convincingly and beyond doubt, to those who were to inherit the promise, the unchangeableness of His purpose and plan, intervened (mediated) with an oath. This was so that by two unchangeable things [His promise and His oath], in which it is impossible for God ever to prove false or deceive us, we who have fled [to Him] for refuge might have mighty indwelling strength and strong encouragement to grasp and hold fast the hope appointed for us and set before [us].

[Now] we have this [hope] as a sure and steadfast anchor of the soul—it cannot slip and it cannot break down under whoever steps out upon it—[a hope] that reaches farther and enters into [the very certainty of the Presence] within the veil, Where Jesus has entered in for us [in advance], a Forerunner having become a High Priest forever after the order [with the rank] of Melchizedek.

Moffatt—For as men swear by a greater than themselves, and as an oath means to them a guarantee that ends any dispute, God, in his desire to afford the heirs of the Promise a special proof of the solid character of his purpose, interposed with an oath; so that by these two solid facts (the Promise and the Oath), where it is impossible for God to be false, we refugees might have strong encouragement to seize the hope set before us, anchoring the soul to it safe and secure, as it enters the inner Presence behind the veil. There Jesus entered for us in advance, when he became high priest for ever with the rank of Melchizedek.

NEB—Men swear by a greater than themselves, and the oath provides a confirmation to end all dispute; and so God, desiring to show even more clearly to the heirs of his promise how unchanging was his purpose, guaranteed it by oath. Here, then, are two irrevocable acts in which God could not possibly play us false, to give powerful encouragement to us, who have claimed his protection by grasping the hope set before us. That hope we hold. It is like an anchor for our lives, an anchor safe and sure. It enters in through the veil, where Jesus has entered on our behalf as forerunner, having become a high priest for ever in the succession of Melchizedek.

Hebrews 7:24-25

KJV—But this (Jesus), because he continueth ever, hath an unchangeable priesthood. Wherefore he is able also to save them to the uttermost that come unto God by him, seeing he ever liveth to make intercession for them.

Amp—But He holds His priesthood unchangeably because He lives on forever. Therefore He is able also to save to the uttermost—completely, perfectly, finally and for all time and eternity—those who come to God through Him, since He is always living to make petition to God and intercede with Him and intervene for them.

Moffatt—He holds his priesthood without any successor, since he continues for ever. Hence for all time he is able to save those who approach God through him, since he is always living to intercede on their behalf.

NEB—But the priesthood which Jesus holds is perpetual, because he remains for ever. That is why he is also able to save absolutely those who approach God through him; he is always living to plead on their behalf.

Hebrews 8:6, 10-12

KJV—But now hath he obtained a more excellent ministry, by how much also he is the mediator of a better covenant, which was established upon better promises.

For this is the covenant that I will make with the house of Israel after those days, saith the Lord; I will put my laws into their mind, and write them in their hearts: and I will be to them a God, and they shall be to me a people: And they shall not teach every man his neighbour, and every man his brother, saying, Know the Lord: for all shall know me, from the least to the greatest. For I will be merciful to their unrighteousness, and their sins and their iniquities will I remember no more.

Amp—But as it now is, He [Christ] has acquired a [priestly] ministry which is as much superior and more excellent [than the old] as the covenant—the agreement—of which He is the Mediator (the Arbiter, Agent) is superior and more excellent; [because] it is enacted and rests upon more important (sublimer, higher and nobler) promises.

For this is the covenant that I will make with the house of Israel after those days, says the Lord: I will imprint My laws upon their minds, even upon their innermost thoughts and understanding, and engrave them upon their hearts, and I will be their God, and they shall be My people. And it will nevermore be necessary for every one to teach his neighbor and his fellow citizen or every one his brother, saying, Know—[that is,] perceive, have knowledge of and get acquainted by experience with—the Lord; for all will know Me, from the smallest to the greatest of them. For I will be merciful and gracious toward their sins and I will remember their deeds of unrighteousness no more.

Moffatt—As it is, however, the divine service he has obtained is superior, owing to the fact that he mediates a superior covenant, enacted with superior promises.

This is the covenant I will make with the house of Israel when that day comes, saith the Lord; I will set my laws within their mind, inscribing them upon their hearts; I will be a God to them, and they shall be a People to me; one citizen will no longer teach his fellow, one man will no longer teach his brother, saying, 'Know the Lord,' for all are to know me, low and high together. I will be merciful to their iniquities, and remember their sins no more.

NEB—But in fact the ministry which has fallen to Jesus is as far superior to theirs as are the covenant he mediates and the promises upon which it is legally secured.

'For the covenant I will make with the house of Israel after those days, says the Lord, is this: I will set my laws in their understanding and write them on their hearts; and I will be their God, and they shall be my people. And they shall not teach one another, saying to brother and fellow-citizen, "Know the Lord!" For all of them, high and low, shall know me; I will be merciful to their wicked deeds, and I will remember their sins no more.'

***

God gave a foreshadowing of our
New Covenant Communion through the
Old Covenant Passover. It delivered God's healing power to those
first Israelites who partook of it.

Exodus 12:3, 5-7

KJV—Speak ye unto all the congregation of Israel, saying, In the tenth day of this month they shall take to them every man a lamb, according to the house of their fathers, a lamb for an house:

Your lamb shall be without blemish, a male of the first year: ye shall take it out from the sheep, or from the goats: And ye shall keep it up until the fourteenth day of the same month: and the whole assembly of the congregation of Israel shall kill it in the evening. And they shall take of the blood, and strike it on the two side posts and on the upper door post of the houses, wherein they shall eat it.

Amp—Tell all the congregation of Israel, On the tenth day of this month they shall take every man a lamb or kid, according to [the size of] the family of which he is the father, a lamb or kid for a house.

Your lamb or kid shall be without blemish, a male of the first year; you shall take it from the sheep or the goats. And you shall keep it until the fourteenth day of the same month; and the whole assembly of the congregation of Israel shall [each] kill [his] lamb in the evening. They shall take of the blood, and put it on the two sideposts and on the lintel [above the door space] of the houses in which they shall eat [the passover lamb].

Moffatt—Tell all the community of Israel that on the tenth day of this month they are each to take a lamb or kid, one lamb for every household.

The Lamb must be a male yearling, unblemished; it may be a lamb or a kid, but you must keep it till the fourteenth day of the month, when every member of the community of Israel shall kill it between sunset and dark. Then they must take some of the blood and smear it on the two door-posts and on the lintel of the house where it is eaten.

NEB—Speak to the whole community of Israel and say to them: On the tenth day of this month let each man take a lamb or a kid for his family, one for each household.

Your lamb or kid must be without blemish, a yearling male. You may take equally a sheep or a goat. You must have it in safe keeping until the fourteenth day of this month, and then all the assembled community of Israel shall slaughter the victim between dusk and dark. They must take some of the blood and smear it on the two door-posts and on the lintel of every house in which they eat the lamb.

Psalm 105:37

KJV—He brought them forth also with silver and gold: and there was not one feeble person among their tribes.

Amp—He brought [Israel] forth also with silver and gold, and there was not one feeble person among their tribes.

Moffatt—Then he led out his clansmen, carrying spoil of gold and silver, not a weary man among them.

NEB—He led Israel out, laden with silver and gold, and among all their tribes no man fell.

1 Corinthians 11:23-26

KJV—For I have received of the Lord that which also I delivered unto you, That the Lord Jesus the same night in which he was betrayed took bread: And when he had given thanks, he brake it, and said, Take, eat: this is my body, which is broken for you: this do in remembrance of me.

After the same manner also he took the cup, when he had supped, saying, This cup is the new testament (or covenant) in my blood: this do ye, as oft as ye drink it, in remembrance of me. For as often as ye eat this bread, and drink this cup, ye do show the Lord's death till he come.

Amp—For I received from the Lord Himself that which I passed on to you—it was given to me personally; that the Lord Jesus on the night when He was treacherously delivered up and while His betrayal was in progress took bread, And when He had given thanks, He broke [it], and said, Take, eat. This is My body which is broken for you. Do this to call Me [affectionately] to remembrance.

Similarly when supper was ended, he took the cup also, saying, This cup is the new covenant [ratified and established] in My blood. Do this, as often as you drink [it], to call Me [affectionately] to remembrance. For every time you eat this bread and drink this cup, you are representing and signifying and proclaiming the fact of the Lord's death until He comes [again].

Moffatt—I passed on to you what I received from the Lord himself, namely, that on the night he was betrayed the Lord Jesus took a loaf, and after thanking God he broke it, saying, 'This means my body broken for you; do this in memory of me.'

In the same way he took the cup after supper, saying, 'This cup means the new covenant ratified by my blood; as often as you drink it, do it in memory of me.' For as often as you eat this loaf and drink this cup, you proclaim the Lord's death until he comes.

NEB—In the same way, he took the cup after supper, and said: 'This cup is the new covenant sealed by my blood. Whenever you drink it, do this as a memorial of me.' For every time you eat this bread and drink the cup, you proclaim the death of the Lord, until he comes.

***

Healing Promises

7

Standing in Faith

If you have faith in your heart and God's Word in your mouth, healing will come. But it may take time for it to manifest in your body. So stand fast in faith, giving thanks to God until it does. Focus on God's Word, not on physical symptoms.

1 John 3:21-22

KJV—Beloved, if our heart condemn us not, then have we confidence toward God. And whatsoever we ask, we receive of him, because we keep his commandments, and do those things that are pleasing in his sight.

Amp—And, beloved, if our consciences (our hearts) do not accuse us—if they do not make us feel guilty and condemn us—we have confidence (complete assurance and boldness) before God; And we receive from Him whatever we ask for, because we (watchfully) obey His orders—observe His suggestions and injunctions, follow His plan for us—and (habitually) practice what is pleasing to Him.

Moffatt—If our heart does not condemn us, beloved, then we have confidence in approaching God, and we get from him whatever we ask, because we obey his commands and do what is pleasing in his sight.

NEB—Dear friends, if our conscience does not condemn us, then we can approach God with confidence, and obtain from him whatever we ask, because we are keeping his commands and doing what he approves.

Hebrews 10:23

KJV—Let us hold fast the profession of our faith without wavering; (for he is faithful that promised;).

Amp—So let us seize and hold fast and retain without wavering the hope we cherish and confess, and our acknowledgement of it, for He Who promised is reliable (sure) and faithful to His word.

Moffatt—Let us hold the hope we avow without wavering (for we can rely on him who gave us the Promise).

NEB—Let us be firm and unswerving in the confession of our hope, for the Giver of the promise may be trusted.

Hebrews 10:35-36

KJV—Cast not away therefore your confidence, which hath great recompense of reward. For ye have need of patience, that, after ye have done the will of God, ye might receive the promise.

Amp—Do not, therefore, fling away your fearless confidence, for it carries a great and glorious compensation of reward. For you have need of steadfast patience and endurance, so that you may perform and fully accomplish the will of God, and thus receive and carry away [and enjoy to the full] what is promised.

Moffatt—Now do not drop that confidence of yours; it carries with it a rich hope of reward. Steady patience is what you need, so that after doing the will of God you may receive what you were promised.

NEB—Do not then throw away your confidence, for it carries a great reward. You need endurance, if you are to do God's will and win what he has promised.

2 Corinthians 10:3-5

KJV—For though we walk in the flesh, we do not war after the flesh: (For the weapons of our warfare are not carnal, but mighty through God to the pulling down of strong holds;) Casting down imaginations, and every high thing that exalteth itself against the knowledge of God, and bringing into captivity every thought to the obedience of Christ.

Amp—For though we walk [live] in the flesh, we are not carrying on our warfare according to the flesh and using mere human weapons. For the weapons of our warfare are not physical (weapons of flesh and blood), but they are mighty before God for the overthrow and destruction of strongholds, [Inasmuch as we] refute arguments and theories and reasonings and every proud and lofty thing that sets itself up against the (true) knowledge of God; and we lead every thought and purpose away captive into the obedience of Christ, the Messiah, the Anointed One.

Moffatt—I do live in the flesh, but I do not make war as the flesh does; the weapons of my warfare are not weapons of the flesh, but divinely strong to demolish fortresses—I demolish theories and any rampart thrown up to resist the knowledge of God, I take every project prisoner to make it obey Christ.

NEB—Weak men we may be, but it is not as such that we fight our battles. The weapons we wield are not merely human, but divinely potent to demolish strongholds; we demolish sophistries and all that rears its proud head against the knowledge of God; we compel every human thought to surrender in obedience to Christ.

Romans 4:16-21

KJV—Therefore it is of faith, that it might be by grace; to the end the promise might be sure to all the seed; not to that only which is of the law, but to that also which is of the faith of Abraham; who is the father of us all, (As it is written, I have made thee a father of many nations,) before him whom he believed, even God, who quickeneth the dead, and calleth those things which be not as though they were. Who against hope believed in hope, that he might become the father of many nations, according to that which was spoken, So shall thy seed be.

And being not weak in faith, he considered not his own body now dead, when he was about an hundred years old, neither yet the deadness of Sarah's womb: He staggered not at the promise of God through unbelief; but was strong in faith, giving glory to God; And being fully persuaded that, what he had promised, he was able also to perform.

Amp—Therefore [inheriting] the promise is the outcome of faith and depends [entirely] on faith, in order that it might be given as an act of grace (unmerited favor), to make it stable and valid and guaranteed to all his descendants; not only to the devotees and adherents of the Law but also to those who share the faith of Abraham, who is [thus] the father of us all, As it is written, I have made you the father of many nations.—He was appointed our father—in the sight of God in Whom he believed, Who gives life to the dead and speaks of the nonexistent things that [He has foretold and promised] as if they [already] existed. [For Abraham, human reason for] hope being gone, hoped on in faith that he should become the father of many nations, as he had been promised, So [numberless] shall your descendants be.

He did not weaken in faith when he considered the [utter] impotence of his own body, which was as good as dead because he was about a hundred years old, or [when he considered] the barrenness of Sarah's (deadened) womb. No unbelief or distrust made him waver or doubtingly question concerning the promise of God, but he grew strong and was empowered by faith as he gave praise and glory to God, Fully satisfied and assured that God was able and mighty to keep His word and to do what He had promised.

Moffatt—That is why all turns upon faith; it is to make the promise a matter of favour, to make it secure for all the offspring, not simply for those who are adherents of the Law but also for those who share the faith of Abraham—of Abraham who is the father of us all (as it is written, I have made you a father of many nations). Such a faith implies the presence of the God in whom he believed, a God who makes the dead live and who calls into being what does not exist. For Abraham, when hope was gone, hoped on in faith, and thus became the father of many nations—even as he was told, So numberless shall your offspring be.

His faith never quailed, even when he noted the utter impotence of his own body (for he was about a hundred years old) or the impotence of Sara's womb; no unbelief made him waver about God's promise; his faith won strength as he gave glory to God and felt convinced that He was able to do what He had promised.

NEB—The promise was made on the ground of faith, in order that it might be a matter of sheer grace, and that it might be valid for all Abraham's posterity, not only for those who hold by the law, but for those also who have the faith of Abraham. For he is the father of us all, as Scripture says: 'I have appointed you to be father of many nations.' This promise, then, was valid before God, the God in whom he put his faith, the God who makes the dead live and summons things that are not yet in existence as if they already were. When hope seemed hopeless, his faith was such that he became 'father of many nations', in agreement with the words which had been spoken to him: 'Thus shall your descendants be.'

Without any weakening of faith he contemplated his own body, as good as dead (for he was about a hundred years old), and the deadness of Sarah's womb, and never doubted God's promise in unbelief, but, strong in faith, gave honour to God, in the firm conviction of his power to do what he had promised.

Hebrews 11:11

KJV—Through faith also Sara herself received strength to conceive seed, and was delivered of a child when she was past age, because she judged him faithful who had promised.

Amp—Because of faith also Sarah herself received physical power to conceive a child, even when she was long past the age for it, because she considered [God] Who had given her the promise, reliable and trustworthy and true to His word.

Moffatt—It was by faith that even Sara got strength to conceive, bearing a son when she was past the age for it—because she considered that she could rely on Him who gave the promise.

NEB—By faith even Sarah herself received strength to conceive, though she was past the age, because she judged that he who had promised would keep faith.

2 Corinthians 12:9

KJV—And he said unto me, My grace is sufficient for thee: for my strength is made perfect in weakness. Most gladly therefore will I rather glory in my infirmities, that the power of Christ may rest upon me.

Amp—But He said to me, My grace—My favor and loving-kindness and mercy—are enough for you, [that is, sufficient against any danger and to enable you to bear the trouble manfully]; for My strength and power are made perfect—fulfilled and completed and show themselves most effective—in [your] weakness. Therefore, I will all the more gladly glory in my weaknesses and infirmities, that the strength and power of Christ, the Messiah, may rest—yes, may pitch a tent [over] and dwell—upon me!

Moffatt—But he told me, "It is enough for you to have my grace: it is in weakness that my power is fully felt." So I am proud to boast of all my weakness, and thus to have the power of Christ resting on my life.

NEB—But his answer was: 'My grace is all you need; power comes to its full strength in weakness.' I shall therefore prefer to find my joy and pride in the very things that are my weakness; and then the power of Christ will come and rest upon me.

Hebrews 4:14-16

KJV—Seeing then that we have a great high priest, that is passed into the heavens, Jesus the Son of God, let us hold fast our profession. For we have not an high priest which cannot be touched with the feeling of our infirmities; but was in all points tempted like as we are, yet without sin. Let us therefore come boldly unto the throne of grace, that we may obtain mercy, and find grace to help in time of need.

Amp—Inasmuch then as we have a great High Priest Who has [already] ascended and passed through the heavens, Jesus the Son of God, let us hold fast our confession [of faith in Him], For we do not have a High Priest Who is unable to understand and sympathize and have a fellow feeling with our weaknesses and infirmities and liability to the assaults of temptation, but One Who has been tempted in every respect as we are, yet without sinning. Let us then fearlessly and confidently and boldly draw near to the throne of grace—the throne of God's unmerited favor [to us sinners]; that we may receive mercy [for our failures] and find grace to help in good time for every need—appropriate help and well-timed help, coming just when we need it.

Moffatt—As we have a great high priest, then, who has

passed through the heavens, Jesus the Son of God, let us hold fast to our confession; for ours is no high priest who cannot have sympathy with our weaknesses, but one who has been tempted in every respect like ourselves, yet without sinning. So let us approach the throne of grace with confidence, that we may receive mercy and find grace to help us in the hour of need.

NEB—Since therefore we have a great high priest who has passed through the heavens, Jesus the Son of God, let us hold fast to the religion we profess. For ours is not a high priest unable to sympathize with our weaknesses, but one who, because of his likeness to us, has been tested every way, only without sin. Let us therefore boldly approach the throne of our gracious God, where we may receive mercy and in his grace find timely help.

Philippians 4:6-7

KJV—Be careful for nothing; but in every thing by prayer and supplication with thanksgiving let your requests be made known unto God. And the peace of God, which passeth all understanding, shall keep your hearts and minds through Christ Jesus.

Amp—Do not fret or have any anxiety about anything, but in every circumstance and in everything by prayer and petition [definite requests] with thanksgiving continue to make your wants known to God. And God's peace [be yours, that tranquil state of a soul assured of its salvation through Christ, and so fearing nothing from God and content with its earthly lot of whatever sort that is, that peace] which transcends all understanding, shall garrison and mount guard over your hearts and minds in Christ Jesus.

Moffatt—Never be anxious, but always make your requests

known to God in prayer and supplication with thanksgiving; so shall God's peace, that surpasses all our dreams, keep guard over your hearts and minds in Christ Jesus.

NEB—The Lord is near; have no anxiety, but in everything make your requests known to God in prayer and petition with thanksgiving. Then the peace of God, which is beyond our utmost understanding, will keep guard over your hearts and your thoughts, in Christ Jesus.

Ephesians 6:10-17

KJV—Finally, my brethren, be strong in the Lord, and in the power of his might. Put on the whole armour of God, that ye may be able to stand against the wiles of the devil. For we wrestle not against flesh and blood, but against principalities, against powers, against the rulers of the darkness of this world, against spiritual wickedness in high places.

Wherefore take unto you the whole armour of God, that ye may be able to withstand in the evil day, and having done all, to stand. Stand therefore, having your loins girt about with truth, and having on the breastplate of righteousness; And your feet shod with the preparation of the gospel of peace; Above all, taking the shield of faith, wherewith ye shall be able to quench all the fiery darts of the wicked. And take the helmet of salvation, and the sword of the Spirit, which is the word of God.

Amp—In conclusion, be strong in the Lord—be empowered through your union with Him; draw your strength from Him—that strength which His [boundless] might provides. Put on God's whole armor—the armor of a heavy-armed soldier, which God supplies—that you may be able successfully to stand up against [all] the strategies and the deceits of the devil. For we are not wrestling with flesh and blood—contending only with physical opponents—but against the despotisms, against the powers, against [the master spirits who are] the world rulers of this present darkness, against the spirit forces of wickedness in the heavenly (supernatural) sphere.

Therefore put on God's complete armor, that you may be able to resist and stand your ground on the evil day [of danger], and having done all [the crisis demands], to stand [firmly in your place]. Stand therefore—hold your ground—having tightened the belt of truth around your loins, and having put on the breastplate of integrity and of moral rectitude and right standing with God; And having shod your feet in preparation [to face the enemy with the firm-footed stability, the promptness and the readiness produced by the good news] of the Gospel of peace. Lift up over all the (covering) shield of saving faith, upon which you can quench all the flaming missiles of the wicked [one]. And take the helmet of salvation and the sword the Spirit wields, which is the Word of God.

Moffatt—To conclude. Be strong in the Lord and in the strength of his might; put on God's armour, so as to be able to stand against the stratagems of the devil. For we have to struggle, not with blood and flesh but with the angelic Rulers, the angelic Authorities, the potentates of the dark present, the spirit-forces of evil in the heavenly sphere.

So take God's armour, that you may be able to make a stand upon the evil day and hold your ground by overcoming all the foe. Hold your ground, tighten the belt of truth about your loins, wear integrity as your coat of mail, and have your feet shod with the stability of the gospel of peace; above all, take faith as your shield, to enable you to quench all the fire-tipped darts flung by the evil one, put on salvation as your helmet, and take the Spirit as your sword (that is, the word of God).

NEB—Finally then, find your strength in the Lord, in his mighty power. Put on all the armour which God provides, so that you may be able to stand firm against the devices of the devil. For our fight is not against human foes, but against cosmic powers, against the authorities and potentates of this dark world, against the superhuman forces of evil in the heavens.

Therefore, take up God's armour; then you will be able to stand your ground when things are at their worst, to complete every task and still to stand. Stand firm, I say. Fasten on the belt of truth; for coat of mail put on integrity; let the shoes on your feet be the gospel of peace, to give you firm footing; and, with all these, take up the great shield of faith, with which you will be able to quench all the flaming arrows of the evil one. Take salvation for helmet; for sword, take that which the Spirit gives you— the words that come from God.

***

Confess
Healing

Holding fast to your
profession of faith—
Hebrews 10:23—means
to hold fast to your
confession. The Greek
word for profession is also
used for confession. The
words of your mouth are
more powerful than you
probably have ever
realized. Confess your
healing...and your health.

Proverbs 18:21

KJV—Death and life are in the power of the tongue: and they that love it shall eat the fruit thereof.

Amp—Death and life are in the power of the tongue, and they who indulge it shall eat the fruit of it [for death or life].

Moffatt—Death and life are determined by the tongue: the talkative must take the consequences.

NEB—The tongue has power of life and death; make friends with it and enjoy its fruits.

Proverbs 10:11

KJV—The mouth of a righteous man is a well of life: but violence covereth the mouth of the wicked.

Amp—The mouth of an [uncompromisingly] righteous man is a well of life, but the mouth of the wicked conceals violence.

Moffatt—The talk of good men is a lifegiving fountain: the talk of bad men overflows with harm.

NEB—The words of good men are a fountain of life; the wicked are choked by their own violence.

Proverbs 13:3

KJV—He that keepeth his mouth keepeth his life: but he that openeth wide his lips shall have destruction.

Amp—He who guards his mouth keeps his life, but he who opens wide his lips will come to ruin.

Moffatt—He guards his life who guards his lips: he who talks freely—it is ruin to him!

NEB—He who minds his words preserves his life; he who talks too much comes to grief.

Proverbs 15:4

KJV—A wholesome tongue is a tree of life: but perverseness therein is a breach in the spirit.

Amp—A gentle tongue [with its healing power] is a tree of life, but willful contrariness in it breaks down the spirit.

Moffatt—A soothing tongue means life and peace, but wild words wound.

NEB—A soothing word is a staff of life, but a mischievous tongue breaks the spirit.

Joel 3:10

KJV—Beat your plowshares into swords, and your pruning hooks into spears: let the weak say, I am strong.

Amp—Beat your plowshares into swords, and your pruning hooks into spears; let the weak say, I am strong—a warrior!

Moffatt—Hammer your ploughshares into swords, your pruning-hooks into lances. Let your weaklings think them warriors, let your cowards think them heroes!

NEB—Beat your mattocks into swords and your pruning-hooks into spears. Rally to each other's help, all you nations round about. Let the weakling say, 'I am strong', and let the coward show himself brave.

James 3:2-6

KJV—For in many things we offend all. If any man offend not in word, the same is a perfect man, and able also to bridle the whole body. Behold, we put bits in the horses' mouths, that they may obey us; and we turn about their whole body. Behold also the ships, which though they be so great, and are driven of fierce winds, yet are they turned about with a very small helm, whithersoever the governor listeth.

Even so the tongue is a little member, and boasteth great things. Behold, how great a matter a little fire kindleth! And the tongue is a fire, a world of iniquity: so is the tongue among our members, that it defileth the whole body, and setteth on fire the course of nature; and it is set on fire of hell.

Amp—For we all often stumble and fall and offend in many things. And if any one does not offend in speech—never says the wrong things—he is a fully developed character and a perfect man, able to control his whole body and to curb his entire nature. If we set bits in the horses' mouths to make them obey us, we can turn their whole bodies about. Likewise look at the ships, though they are so great and are driven by rough winds, they are steered by a very small rudder wherever the impulse of the helmsman determines. Even so the tongue is a little member, and it can boast of great things. See how much wood or how great a forest a tiny spark can set ablaze! And the tongue [is] a fire. [The tongue is a] world of wickedness set among our members, contaminating and depraving the whole body and setting on fire the wheel of birth—the cycle of man's nature—being itself ignited by hell (Gehenna).

Moffatt—We all make many a slip, but whoever avoids slips of speech is a perfect man; he can bridle the whole of the body as well as the tongue. We put bridles into the mouths of horses to make them obey us, and so, you see, we can move the whole of their bodies. Look at ships too; for all their size and speed under stiff winds, they are turned by a tiny rudder wherever the mind of the steersman chooses. So the tongue is a small member of the body, but it can boast of great exploits. What a forest is set ablaze by a little spark of fire! And the tongue is a fire, the tongue proves a very world of mischief among our members, staining the whole of the body and setting fire to the round circle of existence with a flame fed by hell.

NEB—All of us often go wrong; the man who never says a wrong thing is a perfect character, able to bridle his whole being. If we put bits into horses' mouths to make them obey our will, we can direct their whole body. Or think of ships: large they may be, yet even when driven by strong gales they can be directed by a tiny rudder on whatever course the helmsman chooses. So with the tongue. It is a small member but it can make huge claims. What an immense stack of timber can be set ablaze by the tiniest spark! And the tongue is in effect a fire. It represents among our members the world with all its wickedness; it pollutes our whole being; it keeps the wheel of our existence red-hot, and its flames are fed by hell.

Luke 6:45

KJV—A good man out of the good treasure of his heart bringeth forth that which is good; and an evil man out of the evil treasure of his heart bringeth forth that which is evil: for of the abundance of the heart his mouth speaketh.

Amp—The upright (honorable, intrinsically good) man out of the good treasure [stored] in his heart produces what is upright (honorable and intrinsically good); and the evil man out of the evil storehouse brings forth that which is depraved (wicked and intrinsically evil), for out of the abundance (overflow) of the heart his mouth speaks.

Moffatt—The good man produces good from the good stored in his heart, and the evil man evil from his evil: for a man's mouth utters what his heart is full of.

NEB—A good man produces good from the store of good within himself; and an evil man from evil within produces evil. For the words that the mouth utters come from the overflowing of the heart.

***

Healing
Promises

Healing Scriptures

QUICK REFERENCE LIST

142

GLORIA'S SCRIPTURE LIST

Hear and receive my Word and the
years of your life will be many!
(Proverbs 4:10)

Receiving the Word or acting on the Word, and not being a hearer only, comes by being diligent. If you have pressing needs for healing in your body, look up the following verses and read them aloud daily. Refuse to compromise with doubt and unbelief in any form. And remember: God's Word works!

Healing
Promises

Exodus 15:26	**Mark 11:22-24**
Exodus 23:25	**Mark 16:14-18**
Deuteronomy 7:14-15	**Romans 4:16-21**
Deuteronomy 30:19-20	**Romans 8:2, 11**
1 Kings 8:56	**2 Corinthians 10:3-5**
Psalm 91:9-10, 14-16	**Galatians 3:13-14, 29**
Psalm 103:1-5	**Ephesians 6:10-17**
Psalm 107:19-21	**Philippians 2:13**
Psalm 118:17	**Philippians 4:6-7**
Proverbs 4:20-24	**2 Timothy 1:7**
Isaiah 41:10	**Hebrews 10:23**
Isaiah 53:4-5	**Hebrews 10:35-36**
Jeremiah 1:12	**Hebrews 11:11**
Jeremiah 30:17	**Hebrews 13:8**
Joel 3:10	**James 5:14-16**
Nahum 1:9	**1 Peter 2:24**
Matthew 8:2-3	**1 John 3:21-22**
Matthew 8:16-17	**1 John 5:14-15**
Matthew 18:18-19	**3 John 2**
Matthew 21:21	**Revelation 12:11**

Prayer for Salvation and Baptism in the Holy Spirit

Heavenly Father, I come to You in the Name of Jesus. Your Word says, "Whosoever shall call on the name of the Lord shall be saved" (Acts 2:21). I am calling on You. I pray and ask Jesus to come into my heart and be Lord over my life according to Romans 10:9-10: "If thou shalt confess with thy mouth the Lord Jesus, and shalt believe in thine heart that God hath raised him from the dead, thou shalt be saved. For with the heart man believeth unto righteousness; and with the mouth confession is made unto salvation." I do that now. I confess that Jesus is Lord, and I believe in my heart that God raised Him from the dead.

I am now reborn! I am a Christian—a child of Almighty God! I am saved! You also said in Your Word, "If ye then, being evil, know how to give good gifts unto your children: HOW MUCH MORE shall your heavenly Father give the Holy Spirit to them that ask him?" (Luke 11:13). I'm also asking You to fill me with the Holy Spirit. Holy Spirit, rise up within me as I praise God. I fully expect to speak with other tongues as You give me the utterance (Acts 2:4). In Jesus' Name. Amen!

Begin to praise God for filling you with the Holy Spirit. Speak those words and syllables you receive—not in your own language, but the language given to you by the Holy Spirit. You have to use your own voice. God will not force you to speak. Don't be concerned with how it sounds. It is a heavenly language!

Continue with the blessing God has given you and pray in the spirit every day.

You are a born-again, Spirit-filled believer. You'll never be the same!

Find a good church that boldly preaches God's Word and obeys it. Become part of a church family who will love and care for you as you love and care for them.

We need to be connected to each other. It increases our strength in God. It's God's plan for us.

Make it a habit to watch the *Believer's Voice of Victory* television broadcast and become a doer of the Word, who is blessed in his doing (James 1:22-25).

About the Authors

Kenneth and Gloria Copeland are the best-selling authors of more than 60 books. They have also co-authored numerous books including *Family Promises,* the *LifeLine* series and *From Faith to Faith—A Daily Guide to Victory.* As founders of Kenneth Copeland Ministries in Fort Worth, Texas, Kenneth and Gloria have been circling the globe with the uncompromised Word of God since 1967, preaching and teaching a lifestyle of victory for every Christian.

Their daily and Sunday *Believer's Voice of Victory* television broadcasts now air on more than 500 stations around the world, and the *Believer's Voice of Victory* magazine is distributed to nearly 600,000 believers worldwide. Kenneth Copeland Ministries' international prison ministry reaches more than 20,000 new inmates every year and receives more than 20,000 pieces of correspondence each month. Their teaching materials can also be found on the World Wide Web. With offices and staff in the United States, Canada, England, Australia, South Africa, Ukraine and Singapore, Kenneth and Gloria's teaching materials—books, magazines, audios and videos—have been translated into at least 26 languages to reach the world with the love of God.

Believer's Voice of
VICTORY

When The LORD first spoke to Kenneth and Gloria Copeland about starting the *Believer's Voice of Victory* magazine...

He said: *This is your seed. Give it to everyone who ever responds to your ministry, and don't ever allow anyone to pay for a subscription!*

For nearly 40 years, it has been the joy of Kenneth Copeland Ministries to bring the good news to believers. Readers enjoy teaching from ministers who write from lives of living contact with God, and testimonies from believers experiencing victory through God's Word in their everyday lives.

Today, the *BVOV* magazine is mailed monthly, bringing encouragement and blessing to believers around the world. Many even use it as a ministry tool, passing it on to others who desire to know Jesus and grow in their faith!

Request your FREE subscription to the *Believer's Voice of Victory* magazine today!

Go to **freevictory.com** to subscribe online, or call us at **1-800-600-7395** (U.S. only) or **+1-817-852-6000**.

We're Here for You!®

Your growth in God's WORD and victory in Jesus are at the very center of our hearts. In every way God has equipped us, we will help you deal with the issues facing you, so you can be the **victorious overcomer** He has planned for you to be.

The mission of Kenneth Copeland Ministries is about all of us growing and going together. Our prayer is that you will take full advantage of all The LORD has given us to share with you.

Wherever you are in the world, you can watch the *Believer's Voice of Victory* broadcast on television (check your local listings), the Internet at kcm.org or on our digital Roku channel.

Our website, **kcm.org,** gives you access to every resource we've developed for your victory. And, you can find contact information for our international offices in Africa, Asia, Australia, Canada, Europe, Ukraine and our headquarters in the United States.

Each office is staffed with devoted men and women, ready to serve and pray with you. You can contact the worldwide office nearest you for assistance, and you can call us for prayer at our U.S. number, +1-817-852-6000, 24 hours every day!

We encourage you to connect with us often and let us be part of your everyday walk of faith!

Jesus Is LORD!

Kenneth and Gloria Copeland